Gerry Jeffers is an educational researcher, lecturer and writer. He has worked as a lecturer at Maynooth University and is a former national co-ordinator of the Transition Year Curriculum Support Service. He has also worked in schools in Dublin, Kilkenny and Kenya. He is chairperson of the Ubuntu Network, promoting development education in initial teacher education.

*For the Clear family*

# CLEAR
# VISION
## THE LIFE AND LEGACY OF NOEL CLEAR
### Social Justice Champion, 1937 – 2003

### Gerry Jeffers

VERITAS

Published 2017 by
Veritas Publications
7-8 Lower Abbey Street
Dublin 1, Ireland
publications@veritas.ie
www.veritas.ie

ISBN 978 1 84730 804 7

10 9 8 7 6 5 4 3 2 1

A catalogue record for this book is available from the British Library.

Cover features a portrait of Noel Clear by Seán Hayes; designed by
Barbara Croatto, Veritas
Printed in Ireland by SPRINT-print Ltd, Dublin

Veritas books are printed on paper made from the wood pulp of
managed forests. For every tree felled, at least one tree is planted,
thereby renewing natural resources.

# Contents

# Foreword

I am now convinced that I first met Noel Clear in the 1960s. I was a member of the junior table tennis team in the St Vincent de Paul run St Mary's Youth Club in Ballyfermot and we were competing against our counterparts in Inchicore. Even by then Noel Clear – energetic, open – was a leader in the youth club involved. Noel had the innate ability to be a leader without having to be labelled such, without affectation but with great effectiveness.

I then met Noel again in 1984 when I was appointed as a probation officer. Again, you would not know it by his manner, aura or demeanour, Noel Clear was by then second in command of the Probation and Welfare Service – the biggest social work organisation in the country.

In an organisation that was an arm of the Department of Justice, at times it appeared to me that Noel Clear was the human face of the service.

He was approachable, open, considered and capable. He could make tough decisions, it came with the territory, but you never felt they were wrong or unfairly arrived at.

Noel worked in the Probation Service for thirty-seven years, a remarkable achievement – but of course he was working elsewhere as well with his Trojan involvement in the Society of St Vincent de Paul.

It has been well remarked that Noel rose to become president of the massive organisation that is St Vincent de Paul. Noel Clear never rose – it appeared that he floated among people – rising suggests superiority over others – Noel was never comfortable in that position.

In his many years of involvement with the Society of St Vincent de Paul – including six years as national president – he transformed the organisation making it not just a helping agency but an organisation that campaigned and lobbied on behalf of the downtrodden. Today the organisation is an authoritative and respected voice on national issues such as poverty and inequality.

Noel radiated warmth and generosity – I never heard a bad word uttered by him or about him.

He always spoke about people as if they were within earshot – a lovely mantra we should all adopt.

Gerry Jeffers has written a warm, affectionate and deeply accessible biography of a man who possessed all those attributes. That Gerry turned his formidable skills, research and time to a such a detailed biography of Noel Clear tells us a lot about these two friends.

Anyone reading this honourable and noble book about such an honourable and noble man will quickly realise that we need more people like Noel Clear – now more than ever.

When I attended his funeral, it was a sense of shock and loss that hung over the Oblate church in his beloved Inchicore and that Noel should have been taken so young and so soon after his well-deserved retirement.

'Saintly' was a word that rested gently on the tongues of those speaking about Noel, we knew that day we were burying a man of great intelligence who knew that knowledge of water was not just knowing the formula $H_2O$ – but that true knowledge of water is thirst.

*Joe Duffy*
*July 2017*

# Introduction

When my friend Noel Clear died in 2003, I wrote an appreciation which *The Irish Times* and subsequently the *SVP Bulletin,* the magazine of the Society of St Vincent de Paul, published. From time to time after that, various people suggested that a longer account might further illuminate the life of a very special person. This, in turn, led to many interesting conversations about Noel and his times.

The original 2003 appreciation was as follows:

*Noel Clear slipped from life on 8 December, aged sixty-five years, and we are all the poorer for his passing. A gifted organiser, decision-maker and problem solver, Noel also possessed an ocean of compassion. He always looked for the good in people, believed in second, third, fourth and more chances, and never gave up on anyone. Before completing his Leaving Cert. in Westland Row CBS, Noel was already involved in developing a youth club in Keogh Square in his native Inchicore. As a member of the probation and welfare service in the Department of Justice, Noel became a real friend to many young people in trouble with the law. They valued his straight talking, his efforts to find them work and his encouragement to stay away from trouble.*

*By the mid-1960s Noel had become the anchor of an energetic group of volunteers from Inchicore and elsewhere who made up*

*a local conference of the Society of St Vincent de Paul (SVP).
Under the banner of St Vincent's Youth Centre, activities included
club nights, performances of Sean O'Casey's plays, football teams,
summer holidays, Christmas food parcels, literacy classes, The
Link magazine, and, eventually, the building of a new youth
centre. Noel, along with local curate Fr Brian Power, held things
together.*

*A young Anne Braine from Drimnagh soon brought a fresh
vitality to the group. To the delight of many, the busy Noel fell in
love. The pair married in 1972 and Anne became Noel's great pillar
of strength, sharing and supporting his dedicated commitment,
while together they reared a fine family.*

*That St Vincent's youth group was keenly aware that many
youth problems result from blatant social inequalities. Discussion,
analysis and debate often flowed into the small hours. Occasionally
letters were written to politicians, government departments and
newspapers. Few showed any interest. When the discourse drifted
too far from reality, invariably the grounded, quiet-spoken Noel
would issue the challenge: 'Yes, but what are we going to do about
it now? Hungry people can't afford to wait for society to improve!'*

*Noel's grassroots work in Inchicore became a solid
apprenticeship for wider roles within the SVP. When, in 1996, Noel
became the SVP's national president, he set about re-positioning the
society for the challenges ahead. Throughout the economic boom
he was shocked continually by the persistence of poverty amid
plenty. He sought to engage policymakers in thinking strategically
to bring about greater social justice. He was rightly angered to
see so many children in poverty, by educational disadvantage, by
inequalities in health provision, by the marginalisation of refugees
and asylum seekers, and by increased homelessness. Not afraid to
speak out, he did so eloquently and coherently, becoming a forceful
and credible advocate for voiceless people.*

*Within the SVP he spearheaded social policy initiatives, promoted a vision of professionalism in a voluntary organisation and increased youth activities. He travelled the length and breadth of the country to listen to and talk with members, to share his vision of a practical Christian organisation bearing food vouchers in one hand and coherent social justice policies in the other.*

*On top of his work with the probation service and his massive voluntary input to the SVP, Noel was also deeply committed, since his school days, to Irish language and culture. Despite his busy life outside the home, Noel was very much a family man, a loving and committed husband and father. Watching Noel's final year unfold was a moving lesson in love, as husband, wife, and three sons dealt with illness and with each other, with such care and affection.*

*Noel's life of service was the practical expression of a strong Christian belief. To have known him, to have been his friend, was a wonderful privilege. He died wrapped in the loving care of Anne and their sons Rory, Alan and Conor. For them, for his brothers Seán and Tony, and for thousands of others, Noel's passing leaves a void that cannot be filled.*

*Ar dheis Dé go raibh a anam dílis.*

Noel's story spans the years from the enactment of the Irish Constitution to the height of what are referred to as the Celtic Tiger years. He packed a lot into his busy sixty-five years, living through momentous social, economic, cultural and religious changes. The Ireland that he grew up in during the 1940s and 1950s altered dramatically in the latter half of the twentieth century. The dominant Gaelic, nationalist and Catholic perspectives of his school days shifted and stuttered as external and internal forces re-shaped the society. Much of Noel's engagement with paid and voluntary work as an adult was often in response to changing social conditions. As a husband and parent, especially in the

1970s and 1980s, he experienced changing outlooks on family life. Brought up in a staunchly Catholic home, Noel's life began at a time when the Church was a respected and powerful force within Irish society. He lived through the questioning of accepted traditions, particularly following the Second Vatican Council. He witnessed the beginning of the collapse of that authority and credibility as the scandals of child abuse and failed leadership were exposed. Politically, the Troubles, with their attendant violence and suffering, led Noel to re-imagine his nationalism. He also lived through the transition from rationing and highly visible poverty to material and infrastructural transformation; he also observed the conspicuous consumption that characterised Ireland's economy at the turn of the century. By 2003, the Ireland Noel was born into sixty-five years earlier had changed dramatically.

These changes impacted directly on Noel. He lived with many tensions: between his paid work and his voluntary activities; between the demands on his time outside the home and his family life; between his preference for simple practical responses to alleviate poverty and pain, and the inherent bureaucracy of organisations; between his straightforward Christian faith and a Church that sometimes seemed to neglect the truth. Like many others, he struggled to integrate his values, beliefs and practices into a coherent whole. Noel's story and legacy is of a man at a specific time responding to unique circumstances, but it also carries lessons that are timeless and offer inspiration when facing the challenges of today's world.

My own relationship with Noel goes back to the late 1960s when we were both involved with the youth group in Inchicore; we became friends and kept in touch through the years. Shortly after he became SVP national president, Noel invited me to join the social policy group. From our earliest encounters, Noel's compassion, commitment and integrity were very striking. Interviewing people for this book has confirmed the strength of those qualities. I am grateful to all those who gave generously of their time to reflect, reminisce and recall; we had many memorable and moving conversations. Thanks also to those who read drafts of the text and made helpful suggestions. The book is much richer because of them.

*Gerry Jeffers*
*July 2017*

# Chapter 1
## Foundation Years

A baby born at Christmastime brings special joy. For Jack and Úna Clear there was double joy on 24 December 1937 with the birth of identical twins, Seán and Noel, brothers to nineteen month old Tony. At that time the family lived beside the Seventh Lock on the Grand Canal, near Bluebell in south west Dublin. Two years later they moved to Tyrconnell Road, Inchicore where Noel lived, uninterrupted, for the next sixty-three years.

Seán remembers their childhood as a happy, innocent time. From the outset, Noel and Seán were very attached to each other. 'We were so close it was unreal,' recalls Seán. They shared, stuck up for each other, got into trouble together and forged a strong bond that remained throughout life. Seán, who has lived in Galway since the late 1960s, adds that their similarity in tastes and thinking was often very striking. He recalls one Christmas in the 1970s. In Galway, he carefully selected a Johnny McEvoy LP for his twin brother and travelled to Dublin with the present. As Noel opened the package and glimpsed the album cover he pointed to another wrapped gift on the table. Even before he opened it, Seán guessed, correctly, that they had purchased identical presents.

Older brother Tony – currently living in Co. Wicklow and, like Seán, enjoying retirement – confirms the bond. 'The twins,' he remembers, 'were always up to mischief when they were young. 'They were almost telepathic in their communication.' Tony quotes the great novelist John McGahern: 'I was a single star until the twins arrived'[1], and laughs. 'I still have a clear memory of watching the twins in their cot with their bottles. Seán would finish his bottle and then crawl to Noel's end and finish his. They were so close to each other.'

The brothers attended Scoil Mhuire gan Smál primary school beside the Oblate Church on Tyrconnell Road. When teachers have children from the same family to contend with, they often mix up names. Identical twins in the same class pose a special challenge. 'Seán, you sit here at the front; Noel, take the seat at the back,' said the teacher. No sooner was the teacher's back turned than the twins swapped places, adding to the confusion and enjoying the fun. 'Even within the family, there were relatives who weren't sure who was who,' says Tony.

A sense of fairness and the courage to stand up to authority manifested itself at a young age. Seán takes up the story: 'We had a teacher, Mr Dwane. Now he wasn't a bad teacher but like everybody else at that time he used corporal punishment. One day – we were about eight or nine at the time – he called out "Noel Clear. Come up here." Noel was due to get two biffs. We looked at each other. "Come on," I said and we both just got up and walked right out of the classroom and home to our mother.' After much persistence, Úna eventually cajoled the twins into going back to school.

## Church

'The Oblate Church was a big factor in our lives,' remembers Seán. Úna encouraged her sons to go to Mass, to join the sodality. 'We lived almost next door to the church and so going to 7.30am Mass before school was easy. So much was taken for granted then,' he adds. The rhythms and routines of Catholic life were

---

1. John McGahern, *Memoir*, London: Faber and Faber, 2005, p. 6.

central to the Clear household: the sombre December period of Advent gave way to the joyous Christmas season when the crib, in various manifestations, highlighted an amazing story. Lent, when particular privations are embraced voluntarily, was taken seriously. This culminated in an intense week of services, especially on Holy Thursday and Good Friday, prior to Easter Sunday and the celebration of the Resurrection. May, especially in the 1950s, was very much the month of Mary. Processions, which would begin in the church and end outdoors where a statue of Mary was 'crowned' with garlands of flowers, were common throughout Ireland. On the radio and gramophone Fr Sydney MacEwan's rendition of 'Bring Flowers of the Rarest' provided one popular soundtrack to the times. The twins were sixteen years old during the Marian year that ran from December 1953 to 1954. This year of prayers and devotions marked the one hundredth anniversary of the proclamation of the dogma of the Immaculate Conception[2]. Seán recalls that the local processions made a strong impression on Noel and himself. In addition, there were novenas, sodalities and retreats, the Rosary, benediction and the Stations of the Cross. One overall effect, remembers Seán, was a strong belief in the power of prayer. He adds, his eyes twinkling, that this was especially pronounced at exam times! Tony echoes Seán's memories: 'A lot of our life was centred on the church and the grotto[3]. We were all in the sodality. I especially remember the May processions and singing in the choir.'

---

2. It was during that year that many of the Marian shrines and grottos one still sees throughout Ireland were constructed. Marian was also a very popular name for girls born during that year.

3. First built in 1883, following a pilgrimage from Inchicore to Lourdes, the present structure, a replica of the Lourdes grotto, was completed in 1930 and has been a very popular prayer site ever since. Much of the work was done voluntarily by workers at the CIE Works in Inchicore. When the new grotto was blessed by Archbishop Byrne in 1930, it is estimated that about one hundred thousand people were present.

Both Noel's brothers remember their childhoods as times of great freedom. 'Together with our cousins we roamed the Memorial Park [in nearby Islandbridge] and further on, up to the Phoenix Park. In the other direction, the Naas Road then only had houses as far as what is now the Bluebell turn-off. Beyond that were fields, now full of industrial sites running up to the Red Cow Interchange. I'm sure it rained a lot, but I can only remember sunny days,' says Tony.

Children's comics were particularly popular in the 1940s and 1950s; weekly sales of *The Dandy* tipped the two million mark in 1950. Seán and Noel were regular readers of both *The Dandy* and *The Beano,* buying their copies from either Miss Egan's or Miss Maher's, two of the newsagents on Tyrconnell Road.

## Jack and Úna

Noel's grandfather, William Clear, grew up in Co. Kilkenny and moved to Dublin in search of work. At twenty-five years of age, in 1905, he married into a family of publicans, the Murrays. Initially, William and his wife Mary Theresa lived in Ballybough, an inner city enclave of northeast Dublin city. They had two children, John Luke – known as Jack – born in 1908 and Julia – known as Juju – a year later. When the First World War broke out, William, like many others, joined the British Army. William, a member of the Royal Dublin Fusiliers, was dispatched to fight in Turkey. Wounded in battle, he was sent home but, sadly, died shortly afterwards.

Noel's grandmother, Mary Theresa Murray, had inherited one of her father's pubs, beside the Ballyfermot Bridge, the humpback bridge at the Seventh Lock on the Grand Canal. For years it was popularly known as 'Mary Theresa's'. 'One of my earliest memories of Grandma Clear was her giving me a small glass of Guinness – a very small glass – and telling me it was good for me,' recalls Tony.

Noel's father, Jack, was sent as a boarder to the Carmelite boarding school in Clondalkin[4]. When he finished school he helped his mother in the pub. Growing up, Tony, Noel and Seán heard many stories of those days. A favourite was how Jack – a talented, versatile handyman – almost single-handedly built a bungalow beside the pub. That became known as 'the house that Jack built'. Another story featured Jack the strong swimmer. It involved a man who drove his pony and trap over the humpback bridge too quickly. The trap tipped over the wall. Trap, pony and owner ended up in the canal. Jack dived in and pulled the spluttering owner to the bank. He then swam back and, with a knife, began to free the horse from the harness as the unfortunate animal was being dragged under by the trap. Jack heard the voice of the half-drowned owner on the bank shouting, 'Don't cut that harness, it's new.' Ignoring the plea, Jack saved the horse. As Tony tells the story he adds, 'According to my mother, the owner didn't even thank him.'

Unfortunately, Jack and his mother had a falling out over the running of the pub. Jack's sister Juju, along with her husband Christy Roche, moved in and ran the business. Sometime later they sold the pub and bought a riding school in Merrion Hall near Ballsbridge. This was during the war years, the Emergency, and the new venture didn't work out. Juju and Christy moved to England. Jack's mother did give him £500, enough to buy the house in Inchicore.

Noel's maternal grandfather was Daniel Keegan, a cooper who worked at the Guinness brewery at St James' Gate. Daniel and his wife, also Mary Theresa, had four daughters and a son: Lillian, Úna, Theresa, Clare and Joseph. The family lived in Clondalkin. The Clear boys remembered their grandfather, a white haired old man with a large moustache who, when rationing was at its peak during the

---

4. This school, Mount St Joseph's, closed in 1936.

Emergency, would share with his grandchildren butter and sugar snaffled from the meagre rations, usually when their grandmother and her daughters were at the miraculous medal devotions.

The Keegans were a very close-knit family. Remarkably, many of them 'migrated' from Clondalkin to Tyrconnell Road, Inchicore. Noel's grandparents moved into number thirty-six. Two aunts, Clare and Teresa – Auntie T – and their families lived at numbers sixty-four and fourteen respectively.

Summers were special. Noel's aunt Clare regularly rented a holiday home in Laytown, Co. Meath and the bevy of cousins, aunts and uncles were always welcome – Kellys, Whiteheads, Behans and Clears. The Clear boys were delighted with the holiday resort's sandy dunes, expansive beach and, of course, relished the newfound sense of freedom.

Sadly, the only Keegan boy, Joseph, an engineer with the ESB was electrocuted in 1930 – he was in his mid-twenties – while working on the Celbridge Power Station.

After schooling with the Presentation Sisters in Clondalkin, Úna worked in Robert Roberts café on Grafton Street, becoming assistant manager. A talented singer and pianist, Úna was a regular performer at the annual Feis Ceoil and was often called upon to accompany other singers. According to Tony, all the Keegan girls were in love with Jack Clear but it was Úna who won his heart. The couple married in 1934 and purchased the house in Tyrconnell Road.

It was in poor repair. Resourceful Jack set about fixing, painting and papering their new home. During the Emergency, Jack joined the army where he drove an ambulance and was often away from Úna and their three young sons for long stretches. He often told his sons stories based on these experiences. Afterwards, Jack drove a van for Harris's electrical shop and, later, became a CIE bus driver, where he worked until retirement.

On one occasion the talented Jack entered a public competition for the design of a new national public telephone box. 'We all went to some hall in town to see the entries displayed,' remembers Tony. Jack's entry was highly commended and, as a result, Cement Roadstone invited him to interview for a job as a draughtsman. For some reason, he never went. The boys were also very proud of the fact that their father made a guitar, a fully working instrument at which they all tried their hands.

Times were tough, especially during the war years. To supplement their income, the family let the upstairs part of the house. Tony, Noel and Seán shared the front room and the twins were often enthralled by their older brother's storytelling as he spun yarns of pirates, cowboys and other exotic characters.

### On yer bike

Mr and Mrs Williams were next door neighbours. Mr Williams – addressing adults as 'Mr', 'Mrs' or 'Miss' was an important way of showing respect at that time – worked with the legendary Dublin salesman Hector Grey at an open-air stall beside the Ha'penny Bridge. When Mr Williams, who wore a hard hat with a wide brim, decided that his cycling days were behind him, he presented his bicycle, an old style 'sit up and beg' type, to the Clear family. Tony, the eldest, became the proud owner of Mr Williams' bicycle. Soon afterwards he set out on an adventure, travelling beyond Palmerstown, Lucan and Leixlip as far as Maynooth in Co. Kildare. However, on the way home, Tony got lost. This episode greatly diminished his enthusiasm for cycling and the bicycle was passed on to the twins.

'Noel and myself had great fun with that bike,' remembers Seán. 'We invented our own cycle track around the laburnum bush in the back garden and competed with each other. Ten lap time-trials were very popular.' And so, a lifelong interest in cycling was nurtured.

Brand new bicycles were among the first purchases the twins made when they began full-time employment. These bikes opened up the countryside and Seán and Noel enjoyed many excursions to Wicklow, Meath, Kildare and beyond. A particularly memorable road adventure took them all around Ireland, staying in An Óige youth hostels.

While neither joined a cycling club, they shared a lifelong fascination with cycle racing. Both witnessed the start of the first ever Rás Tailteann in 1953. Each summer they followed the heroic achievements of Fausto Coppi, Jacques Anquetil, Eddy Merckx and others. Shay Elliott, the first Irishman to win a stage in the Tour de France and to wear the race leader's yellow jersey, was an early hero. The twins felt a particular thrill when, in the 1980s, Stephen Roche, Seán Kelly and Martin Earley showed what Irish cyclists could achieve. And when the Tour de France came to Ireland in 1998, Seán, Noel and Noel's son Alan watched the prologue time-trial whizz through Dublin's streets. Indeed, so enthused was Noel by *Le Tour* that year that he was on the roadside the following day to glimpse the peleton wind its way through the Dublin and Wicklow mountains. The next day Noel and Anne drove to Carrick-on-Suir to view the stage from Enniscorthy to Cork from Seán Kelly Square.

Tony and Seán recall their childhoods with Noel very fondly, a carefree, fun time when, despite limited resources, they, in the company of family dog Spot and many of their cousins, indulged their imaginations and made the most of their situation and surroundings. Memories of their parents are especially affectionate. Tony says, 'Looking back, I know that we could not have had two more beautiful people as parents.'

# Chapter 2
## To School in Westland Row

Tony attended secondary school in Synge Street Christian Brothers School. Seeking to follow in their big brother's footsteps, Noel and Seán sat the Synge Street entrance test. In those days before 'free' secondary education, places were limited and competition tough, especially for a prestigious school like 'Synger'. The results presented the family with a predicament. The school offered Seán a place but not Noel. The twins, however, were not for separation. They applied successfully to another Christian Brothers' School, this time in Westland Row. As well as being reputable, the school was on the number twenty-one bus route from Inchicore, an important practical consideration for Úna and Jack.

Secondary school was manageable; no further classroom walkouts were recorded. Games presented the twins with some challenges, especially on Tuesdays. Apart from cycling, Noel showed little interest in sports. Seán, who shared his brother's views, jokes that, where sport was concerned, limited interest was matched by limited aptitude. Each Tuesday afternoon all boys were expected to report to the sports grounds in Ringsend where Brother Hickey enthusiastically promoted Gaelic football. Seán describes the twins' attitudes: 'We didn't want to be there, but the alternative of sitting in the classroom was even less appealing, so we went.' Putting up with compulsory games was not without rewards. One year, both Noel and Seán found themselves on a team that won the annual seven-a-side tournament. The following year, Brother Hickey's rallying call throughout the school was, 'The Clears got medals last year for standing in front of the goalposts, so I want you all down there next Tuesday.'

In contrast to their sporting achievements, Noel and Seán both shone on the stage, particularly in their final year. In 1955, Brother Tadhg O Muimhneacháin, the school principal, decided that the annual pageant would focus on the lives of the Pearse brothers. Padraig and Willie Pearse were past students of Westland Row CBS, having attended there in the 1890s. Noel and Seán, along with many other 1950s schoolchildren, were familiar with the lives of the Pearse brothers, specifically their nationalism; their participation in the Gaelic League; Padraig's editing of *An Claidheamh Soluis* (the Sword of Light); the founding of St Enda's School in 1908; engagement with the Irish Republican Brotherhood (IRB); Padraig's oration in 1915 at the grave of O'Donovan Rossa and more. Everyone in Westland Row CBS also knew of the brothers' involvement in the 1916 Rising and their subsequent executions[1].

For the 1955 pageant Brother O Muimhneacháin cast the de Cléir[2] brothers in the lead roles, Seán playing Pádraig and Noel as his younger brother Willie. Reviewing the performance in the Dagg Hall,[3] the *Evening Press* observed that *And Green Their*

---

1. In 1966, fifty years after the Rising, the railway station at Westland Row, next door to the school, was renamed Pearse Station.

2. Using the Irish form of their names is one example of how seriously both Seán and Noel regarded their heritage. Noel frequently signed himself 'Nollaig de Cléir' and Seán has always used the Irish form of his name.

3. The Dagg Hall was a theatre space housed in the Royal Irish Academy of Music on Westland Row, adjacent to the CBS school. In 2002 it was renamed the Katherine Brennan Hall.

*Memory* dramatised 'the outstanding incidents of the 1916 Rising from the signing of the Proclamation to the executions of the patriot brothers. The report noted that the boys of Westland Row CBS displayed 'some highly promising talent.' Noel's role included reciting Padraig Pearse's poem 'The Mother'. His performance so impressed one audience member, the writer Sinéad Bean de Valera – who was also the Taoiseach's wife – that she subsequently sent Noel a book token, an early recognition of his potential as a public speaker.

Seán says that Br Tadhg O Muimhneacháin, who later became Provincial of the Irish Christian Brothers, was a major influence on both of them[4]. Noel's interest led to him becoming secretary of the Brothers' Pearse Commemoration Committee in 1958. This responsibility gave Noel opportunities to demonstrate and develop his organising skills. Among other activities, that committee, chaired by Dominican priest An tAthair T. Breathnach, marked the fiftieth anniversary of St Enda's School with a concert in the Gresham Hotel.

Seán remarks that Noel and himself were in secondary school thirty-five to forty years after the 1916 Rising had taken place. 'The embers were still burning,' he says. 'Both of us were inspired by the activities of lads like Seán South of Garryowen, Phil Clarke and the Christles[5]. We often attended republican rallies in the GPO to hear the speeches and put a few pence in the collection

---

4. Some frank extracts from Tadgh O Muimhneacháin's memoirs appeared in *The Irish Times*, 25 September 1985.

5. Sean South was an IRA volunteer, killed in 1957 while attacking an RUC station in Co. Fermanagh, and remembered in the popular song 'Sean South of Garryowen'. Philip Clarke was a member of the IRA who, while serving a prison sentence, was elected to the Westminster Parliament in 1955 on an abstentionist ticket. The Christles were a well-known republican family; Joe Christle was especially prominent in the 1950s campaigns. He later had a distinguished career in cycling, boxing and as a barrister.

box. We would scamper home before the Gardaí started taking names of suspects, fearing we would be arrested.'

Like many others, Noel and Seán found their republican beliefs challenged following the outbreak of the Troubles in the late 1960s. Both were sickened by the violence and the loss of life. They felt that the memories of the heroes of their youth had been tarnished and their support for republicanism waned.

## Corporal punishment

In many all-boys schools during the 1950s – and later – corporal punishment was administered routinely, often for trivial misdemeanours or when a student failed to supply the expected answer to a question.[6] In Westland Row, as elsewhere, the preferred weapon was the leather strap. Typically, the strap consisted of two strips of pliable leather about an inch wide and maybe twelve inches long, machine stitched together with one end tapered to ensure ease of grip. Students had to hold out their hand and receive two, four or even six 'biffs'. This ritual took place in front of the rest of the class with the sound of the 'slap' ringing around the classroom. The pain varied depending on the speed with which the leather made contact with the flesh as well as the location of the impact. Often, a stinging pain was accompanied by a red impression of the leather's neatly stitched shape that lasted for about an hour.

Noel, with his instinctive sense of fairness, regarded this practice unfavourably and, one day, relieved one of his teachers of the leather. That strap, now over sixty years old and fraying at the edges, has become a family heirloom in the Clear household,

---

6. Published accounts by those who attended all-boys school at that time capture some of the fear and casual violence that pervaded many classrooms. One analysis of such accounts can be found at *http://www.erpjournal.net/wp-content/uploads/2017/01/05_ERPV43_Jeffers_2016.pdf*

a relic of a different era and a pointer to Noel's inclination to take action in the face of injustice.

For the teenage twins, there was more to life than school. The Inchicore cinema was further down Tyrconnell Road. 'We often went to the Sunday afternoon matinees,' recalls Seán. 'Noel and myself were big fans of westerns, especially if John Wayne was in them,' he says.

Overall, Noel valued his school days. He developed a lifelong *grá* for the Irish language, took subjects like history and religious education seriously, though was always quick to point to Seán's more scholarly inclinations. The school worked hard at shaping identities that were Catholic, Gaelic and nationalist. In the senior years, in particular, logical thinking about 'big ideas' was encouraged. One classmate, Liam Keegan, has a vivid recollection of being introduced to Catholic social teaching, notably the encyclicals *Rerum Novarum*[7] and *Quadragesimo Anno*.[8] They offered a framework for the teenage boys in Westland Row CBS to engage with ideas related to workers' rights, human freedom and dignity, capitalism, communism and the general social and economic order, ethical behaviour, solidarity and subsidiarity. 'Those classes were very stimulating and had a deep effect on many of us,' remembers Liam.

---

7. 1891 Encyclical Letter of Pope Leo XIII; the title *Rerum Novarum* derives from the first two Lain words, literally 'of revolutionary change'. It highlights the rights and responsibilities of labour and capital, the common good and the role of the state.

8. Pope Pius XI issued this encyclical letter in 1931. *Quadragesimo Anno* refers to 'In the fortieth year'. The letter marked the anniversary of *Rerum Novarum*. Written in the context of the 1929 economic crash, its focus was on social and economic order.

# Chapter 3
## Responding to a Local Need

When Noel Clear was a teenager, collective memory of the independent Ireland that had emerged in the 1920s remained vivid. In many ways, this was a mutually re-enforcing consensus between the new state and the Catholic Church. Historian Louise Fuller remarks:

> The church-state consensus that evolved after independence has to be understood against a backdrop of historico-political developments in the centuries before independence. The Irish Catholic Church had survived through the seventeenth, eighteenth and nineteenth centuries in the face of well-nigh overwhelming odds – plantation, the discrimination of the Penal Laws, persecution – and had emerged victorious.[1]

The consensus can be seen, for example, in the 1935 St Patrick's Day radio broadcast to the United States by Taoiseach Éamon de Valera. He told his American audience:

---

1. L. Fuller, *Irish Catholicism since 1950: The Undoing of a Culture*, Dublin: Gill and Macmillan, 2002, p. 3.

Since the coming of St Patrick, fifteen hundred years ago, Ireland has been a Christian and a Catholic nation. All the ruthless attempts made through the centuries to force her from this allegiance have not shaken her faith. She remains a Catholic nation.[2]

A close overlap of Irish and Catholic identities continued into the 1950s and beyond. Like thousands of young people in the 1950s, Noel joined the Legion of Mary while still at school. The Legion is a voluntary, lay, Catholic organisation which was founded by Frank Duff in Francis Street, Dublin in 1921.[3] It had expanded spectacularly during the following three decades. Its membership was wide ranging and included public intellectuals as well as women and men with little formal schooling.

The Legion of Mary aims to enable the spiritual and social welfare of individual members through prayer and apostolic works.[4] In a typical parish this includes the visiting of families, especially the sick, and carrying out other works of mercy and charity. The Legion developed from a view that sees life as a struggle between light and darkness, good and evil. These opposing forces are personified by Satan and his legionnaires on the one hand and Mary, the mother of Jesus on the other. With Mary as Queen, the Legion adopts the terminology of the army of ancient Rome, highlighting values of loyalty, courage and discipline. The local parish unit is a praesidium and individual

---

2. *Irish Press*, 18 March 1935, quoted in Fuller (2002), p. 5.

3. See, for example, Finola Kennedy's *Frank Duff – A Life Story*, published by Continuum in 2011.

4. In the official handbook, the object of the Legion of Mary is 'the Glory of God through the holiness of its members developed by prayer and active co-operation, under ecclesiastical guidance in Mary's and the Church's work of crushing the head of the serpent and advancing the reign of Christ' The revised, 2005 edition of *Legio Mariae* is available at *www.legionofmary.ie/publications*

members are legionaries. Typically, a praesidium meets weekly and members pray and discuss progress reports. The Legion aims to nurture the spirit of Mary – humble, responsive, faithful and loving – and legionnaires are expected to carry out weekly apostolic work. As with any similar organisation, there was a strong social dimension to the Legion and lasting friendships often blossomed.

In the years prior to the Second Vatican Council, the Church sometimes described itself in militaristic terms. For example, Christians on earth were referred to as 'The Church Militant', while those who had died and gone to heaven made up 'The Church Triumphant'. The Legion is a manifestation of how an integrated social activism forms an essential part of the Church's mission. Spectacular growth of the Legion in Ireland was accompanied by Legion envoys establishing the movement across the world. Today, the Legion of Mary plays a key role in many local Churches, including in Nigeria, South Korea, The Philippines, Brazil and Australia. It is estimated that there is a Legion presence in over one hundred and seventy countries.

Noel joined a praesidium in St Michael's Parish, Inchicore which concentrated its efforts on Keogh Square, a particularly disadvantaged setting.[5] Through this group Noel first met Jerry O'Sullivan. The encounter transformed both their lives.

---

5. Originally Richmond Barracks, a British infantry garrison base built in 1810, Kehoe/Keogh Square was converted into housing units by Dublin Corporation in 1924. From the 1930s onwards a corporation policy was to move those evicted for not paying rent elsewhere to Keogh Square. A fascinating account of the Square, including dozens of photographs, can be found in Liam O'Meara's 2016 book *Who Remembers Keogh Square?* (Riposte Books).

## Noel and the man from Clonakilty

Jerry O'Sullivan was from Clonakilty in Co. Cork. Following secondary school in Rockwell College, Jerry came to Dublin seeking work. His aunt, Mrs Dunlea, lived in Inchicore and he stayed with her. Initially, Jerry found the capital city a lonely place. Working by day, he attended night classes in the College of Commerce, Rathmines. One evening, returning from Rathmines, he dropped in to the Oblate Church, asking the sacristan if he knew anything about the Legion of Mary. The sacristan pointed out two legionnaires in prayer and introduced Jerry to them. They invited him to their weekly meeting in nearby Keogh Square. There Jerry first met Noel who went on to become 'the closest friend I ever had'.

The appalling poverty Jerry and Noel witnessed in the Square shocked them. Large families living in cramped, damp conditions with limited food, poor clothing and footwear and few prospects; the plight of these residents left an indelible impression on both Jerry and Noel. They felt compelled to take action to alleviate its impact on young people. 'We quickly saw that we had to do something,' recalls Jerry, 'commit ourselves to opening a youth club, get to know the parents of these youths, do something about getting them employment, help put some happiness into their lives, get them involved in sport, become their friends.'

For Noel and Jerry, St Vincent's Boys' Club, which they founded, became a shared passion. Energetically and enthusiastically, they worked hard at every idea that seemed reasonable. Football became central as many boys were interested and talented. They also organised Saturday night dances because many young adults found the cost of commercial dancehalls prohibitive. Soon they were acting as advocates. 'Every time one of them got into trouble with the law, we went to the courts and pleaded with the judges for the benefit of the boys or girls affected,' says Jerry.

According to Jerry, this was very satisfying work. They saw themselves as witnesses to what Frank Duff, the Legion of Mary founder, called 'miracles on tap'.[6] It became common practice for Noel and Jerry, after closing the club, to walk up to the grotto in the Oblate Church and pray the Rosary together.

Jerry subsequently went to South America as a Legion of Mary envoy. He became an expert in communications, lectured at the Catholic University in Caracas and advised the Bishops' Conference of Venezuela. His memory stretches back over decades recalling some of those who shared the voluntary work in Inchicore: Paddy Dowling, Paddy Dargan, Maurice Callanan but his conversation continually returns to his friend Noel.

## The Cousin

One of Noel's first cousins, Joe Kelly, lived further down Tyrconnell Road. Joe remembers Noel's involvement with the Legion of Mary as fully committed. 'He was very concerned with the plight of the families in Keogh Square. He had great empathy for people,' says Joe. 'He invited me to get involved.'

Joe, two years older than Noel, was working in a bank at the time and studying at university by night. 'However, Noel was persuasive and I went along, became a member of the Legion of Mary and can truly say that changed my life.' Joe became president of the intermediate praesidium of the Legion in the parish, doing door-to-door visits in Keogh Square. Joe's own story is also fascinating. He sees his involvement with the Legion of Mary as one of a series of decisions and coincidences that led him to consider becoming a priest. In 1960, at the age of twenty-five, Joe entered the Spiritan (Holy Ghost Fathers) novitiate

---

6. *Miracles on Tap* is the title of Frank Duff's account of the early work of the Legion of Mary in Dublin in the 1920s, in particular the miraculous transformation of the lives of some people in Dublin's inner city. The book was published in 1961 by Montfort Publications, New York.

in Kilshane, Co. Tipperary. Six years later Joe Kelly CSSp was ordained a priest in Kimmage Manor. Noel was among those present at the ceremony. For the following half century, Joe, a wise teacher, counsellor and pastor, worked as a priest in Canada.

# Chapter 4
# A Depressed Decade

From the vantage point of post-Celtic Tiger Ireland, it can be difficult to appreciate the hardship experienced by many in the Ireland of the 1950s. Historians, political analysts and other commentators[1] recall an atmosphere of depression, unemployment and emigration. The economic disaster of the mid-1950s is likened to a cancer, eating away at Irish confidence. In 1958 alone, nearly sixty thousand people emigrated.

Since Catholic Emancipation in 1829, the influence of the Catholic Church had been growing. Bishops were regarded as credible leaders of the people. Following independence, political leaders of the new state recognised the Church's standing and sought to co-operate with Church leaders. Much responsibility for health, education and social services was devolved to Catholic groups. By the 1950s, the hierarchy was particularly influential.

1. For example, Lee, J.J. *Ireland 1912-85: Politics and Society*, Cambridge University Press, 1989; Ferriter, D. *The Transformation of Ireland 1900 – 2000*, London: Pearson, 2004; Garvin, T. *Preventing the Future: Why was Ireland so Poor for so long?* Dublin: Gill and Macmillan, 2004. Cooney, J. *John Charles McQuaid: Ruler of Catholic Ireland*, Dublin: The O'Brien Press, 1999. Kenny, M. *Goodbye to Catholic Ireland*, Dublin: New Island Press, 2000; Fuller, L. *Irish Catholicism since 1950: The Undoing of a Culture*, Dublin: Gill and Macmillan, 2002.

Newspapers frequently reported bishops' sermons and pastoral letters in detail. In political and other circles, people spoke of fearing 'a belt of the crozier'. The Archbishop of Dublin, John Charles McQuaid was especially influential, carefully monitoring many aspects of Church life in his diocese.

Religious observance was high. While some reported experiencing the Church as overbearing and stifling, for others their faith and religious practice was a strong, sustaining force. The neighbourhood church was a central feature of many Dubliners' lives. A strong belief in God and commitment to offering practical help to others, especially people in difficulties, were commonly shared values.

Some accounts of the 1950s can be simplistic and reductionist, caricaturing the Church and the times. In reality, people struggled with the complexity of their lives, as they do today. Experiences of the Church varied. Historian Diarmaid Ferriter remarks that the Church 'usually interpreted as monolithic and unyielding with a vice-like grip on all, did not in reality invoke a common reaction, or indeed, faith, on the part of its audience'[2]. Ferriter says that 'acknowledging the diversity of the private experience of Irish Catholicism is important'. While the Church offered Noel a context and worldview that he embraced enthusiastically, he didn't abandon his critical faculties. More than once, Noel's relationship with clerical leadership within the Church became strained. He was especially distrustful of any signs of triumphalism, an apparently unfortunate side effect of high levels of religious observance.

Cultural historian Brian Fallon[3] also warns against a simplistic view of the past. He is critical of what he calls the 'demonisation' of the period between 1930 and 1960. He contrasts

---

2. D. Ferriter, *The Transformation of Ireland 1900–2000*, London: Pearson, 2004, p. 518.

3. Brian Fallon, *An Age of Innocence, Irish Culture 1930–1960*, Dublin: Gill and Macmillan, 1998, p. 3.

the 'unthinking anti-clericalism' of today with a time when the authority of the Catholic Church was rarely questioned seriously by the great majority. As he puts it: 'the coin has been flipped to come down heads instead of tails – but it remains the same well worn coin.' Fallon also states, 'How much more intelligent, and more constructive, it is to come to terms creatively with the past than to amputate it like a diseased limb, or put it under interdict! .... there appears to be a definite pre-conceived *a priori* agenda at work here, a psychological need to paint the present in even brighter colours by correspondingly blackening the past.'

## Key values

For some teenagers like Noel, their religious upbringing through home, school and parish nurtured their idealism. The teaching of Jesus, with its emphasis on a call to living according to clearly stated values, had a strong appeal. Noel liked the clarity and relative simplicity of the Beatitudes. They provided a framework for relating to people and the world around him. The Sermon on the Mount was relevant to Noel's life in Inchicore, especially his work in Keogh Square.

> And opening his mouth he taught them, saying: Blessed are the poor in spirit: for theirs is the kingdom of heaven. Blessed are the meek: for they shall possess the land. Blessed are they that mourn: for they shall be comforted. Blessed are they that hunger and thirst after justice: for they shall have their fill. Blessed are the merciful: for they shall obtain mercy. Blessed are the clean of heart: they shall see God. Blessed are the peacemakers: for they shall be called the children of God. (Mt 5:4–9)

Noel would have drawn strength from Jesus' development of these themes and his warning that adopting these values may well lead one into difficulties.

Blessed are they that suffer persecution for justice sake: for theirs is the kingdom of heaven. Blessed are you when they shall revile you, and persecute you, and speak all that is evil against you, untruly, for my sake: Be glad and rejoice for your reward is very great in heaven. For so they persecuted the prophets that were before you. (Mt 5:10–12)

Noel and Jerry were galvanised by the idea of being witnesses, as lay people and legionnaires, to these values, aware of the challenges Jesus posed:

You are the salt of the earth. But if the salt lose its savour, wherewith shall it be salted? It is good for nothing anymore but to be cast out, and to be trodden on by men. You are the light of the world. A city seated on a mountain cannot be hid. Neither do men light a candle and put it under a bushel, but upon a candlestick, that it may shine to all that are in the house. So let your light shine before men, that they may see your good works, and glorify your Father who is in heaven. (Mt 5:13–16)

As home, school and Sunday sermons elaborated on this core message, Noel's commitment strengthened. He saw the Church continuing the mission of Jesus in concrete ways. The Legion offered a response to the poverty on his doorstep, visiting and befriending people, giving practical help, especially through youth work.

## Squalor

Teresita Durkan offers a telling perspective on the times. Born in Co. Mayo in 1937, the same year as Noel, she joined the Sisters of Mercy and later became president of Carysfort College. In *Goldenbridge: A View from Valparaiso*[4], she recalls her first sight of Inchicore in 1954. Contrasting this part of Dublin with the great, bleak rugged beauty of West Mayo, she remembers decay and poverty. She writes:

> In the 1950s the country was poor. The people who lived in central Dublin were, most of them, poor. The graceful buildings of the Royal Hospital Kilmainham were decayed and filled with storehouse clutter. The Luytens Memorial Park in Islandbridge, built to commemorate the Irishmen who died in the First World War, had been allowed to sink into ruin and neglect. Kilmainham Goal, high on its escarpment, was an unroofed grey shell. Richmond Barracks housed the squalor of Keogh Square. The South Dublin Union was still, in effect, the Poor House, though it was called St Kevin's Hospital. That was the kind of Dublin 8 that I had come to know in the 1950s.

Noel, driven by a strong sense of public service as well as religious faith, became persistently single-minded in the mission of alleviating his neighbours' poverty. At that time there was nothing like the social services that operate today; the Church provided many charitable services, often through volunteers like Noel.

## Origins of St Vincent's Club

A 1962 brochure published to mark the opening of a new premises for St Vincent's Boys' Club recalls some of the history.

---

4. Teresita Durkan, *Goldenbridge: A View from Valparaiso*, Dublin: Veritas, 1997, p. 105.

During the summer of 1958, in answer to repeated requests from the boys of the area, the members of the Legion of Mary praesidium of Our Lady of Perpetual Succour began organising football matches, bicycle tours, outings, etc. Little did they realise what their first efforts would lead to, but it was not until September 1959 that indoor activities began at 51E Keogh Square.

51E is the smallest flat in the Square. It is so small, in fact, that it was impossible to play any games. Yet it was soon to house the biggest family. A break came in 1960 when number eighty-nine became vacant. Through the summer months boys and leaders worked non-stop to paint and prepare their new premises, and when on 22 August they were officially opened they were the pride of the Square.

Bigger and bigger grew that united, happy family, and soon an acute accommodation problem developed again. Finally, when early this year these premises became vacant no effort was spared until that priceless key became our possession.

The boys' club was a modest project. It provided a focal point, a meeting place and some structured recreational activities organised by well-intentioned and enthusiastic adults. Many of these adults, like Noel and Jerry, were still in their twenties and they formed strong and warm relationships with club members.

The Keogh Square environment was tough. In many families, there was no one in paid employment. Money and sometimes food were scarce. The overall fabric of the cold, draughty, leaking buildings was poor. Toilets were often shared between families. There were no televisions or telephones. Black and white photographs from the time often illustrate poorly clad and undernourished children.[5] Smart phones, social media, televised

5. L. O'Meara, *Who Remembers Keogh Square?* Inchicore, Dublin: Riposte Books, 2016.

premiership football, PlayStations or mass foreign holidays had yet to be invented. Knowledge and experience of the world beyond Inchicore was limited. Hence, while a modest project, the club was a bright light in a dark world for many Keogh Square teenagers.

## Emigration

At that time of economic stagnation, the emigrant boat often appeared as an attractive escape route. Many from Inchicore went to England. As was the case for countless other Irish women and men, limited formal education combined with insufficient finance and poor support networks to intensify the challenges they faced in unfamiliar environments. As a practical response, Jerry and Noel began corresponding with some young emigrants. Next, they travelled to London, Birmingham and Manchester to see how former club members were faring. Almost invariably these young people were living in rough circumstances. Some were ill. Jerry still remembers the 'sad and lonely boarding houses in the slums of English cities. Young boys sometimes lived in terrible conditions, and in real danger. We promised to do our best to find them employment back in Dublin, helped pay their way back home and make contact with their families.'

Back home, *The Link*, a small, home produced monthly magazine, offered one response to this situation. It contained news snippets, advice and suggestions that, in a pre-internet era, maintained a valuable link with home. Early issues of the *The Link* include a fictionalised serial following the exploits of two Dublin eighteen year olds who take the emigrant boat to Holyhead. From the early 1960s copies were posted to former club members across Britain. Back copies of *The Link* offer telling insights into Noel's thinking on many topics and how he viewed youth and social issues.

# Chapter 5
# The Young Worker

'I remember when we got our Leaving Cert results,' recalls Seán. 'In those days, well before the CAO system, the slip of paper came in the post. We both passed and were pleased with that. But neither of us had enough marks to get the well-regarded jobs in the civil service, the corporation, the ESB, that sort of thing. Anyway, we didn't have too much time either to celebrate or be disappointed because at four o'clock on that day we were due to take a bunch of lads from Keogh Square to see Chipperfield's Circus up near the North Circular Road.'

Some months earlier, the twins had decided that, Leaving Cert results notwithstanding, they would attempt to line up employment of some description. Around Christmas they took to writing to many of the big Dublin firms such as Hughes Brothers; Johnston, Mooney and O'Brien; Kelloggs; and Kennedy's Bakery on Parnell Street. During the Leaving Cert, in June 1956, a letter arrived inviting both to an interview in Kennedy's. Mr Peter Kennedy, the proprietor, interviewed Noel and Seán. The twins impressed their interviewer and he offered them jobs. 'Just bring a pen. That's all you need,' pronounced the bakery boss. Armed with their new pens, they began work as clerical officers the following Monday. 'Fortunately,' adds Seán, 'neither of us was a day unemployed until we retired.'

Kennedy's had a fleet of distinctive vans, with drivers delivering bread from the bakery throughout the city and into the developing suburbs. The new recruits' tasks included liaison with the van drivers, and checking and reconciling volume sold with quantities remaining. Seán and Noel were quick with figures and good with people. 'But you had to wait until the last van came in. That could have been 7pm or 7.30pm and maybe even as late as ten pm on a Saturday,' explains Seán. Noel took to describing themselves as 'the bread slaves', conscious that unpaid overtime at work was keeping him from the boys' club. However, the pay of five pounds and ten shillings per week was higher than the equivalent positions in the civil service. There were also bonuses at Christmas so they didn't complain too vociferously. The atmosphere was pleasant, even if, like many other workplaces then, it was run on paternalistic lines with Peter Kennedy 'like a well-intentioned headmaster'. While working in Kennedy's, Seán and Noel encountered many 'characters', including the well-known comedian Jack Cruise[1].

The following summer, on holidays from the bakery, the twin brothers headed off on their bicycles to explore the Irish countryside through the network of An Óige youth hostels. 'It was a great holiday,' remembers Seán, recounting how Noel insisted on having an Irish tricolour sticker on his mudguard. North of the border, the boys were stopped by members of the Royal Ulster Constabulary (RUC) and quizzed about the sticker. 'We were released without charge,' laughs Seán.

---

1. Dubliner Jack Cruise, born 1915, was a popular stage actor and comedian in an era before Ireland had a national television station. One of his best known creations was John Joe Mahockey from Ballyslapdashamuckery, a shrewd countryman, or, to use the Dublin expression, a 'culchie'.

## How do you run a boys' club?

While delighted to be in paid employment, Noel's real passion was his evening and weekend work with Jerry in the boys' club. With little formal training available for club volunteers, they learned mainly through experience, talking to each other and occasional reading.

In the 1950s, dominant ideas about boys' clubs were often framed in terms of Christian charity. A 1948 Belvedere Newsboys Club booklet, *Boys: A Plan to Help Them,* doesn't mince its words in describing living conditions in the city.

Parts of the slums of Dublin are amongst the worst in Europe; great numbers of men and women are born there, multiply and die amid conditions that cannot soberly be described. These slum-dwellers are the heart of Dublin. The slums are made up of a heterogenous mass of people of as many varying grades of poverty as there are grades of wealth in a middle-class suburb. Many families have two-room tenements; many have three and four-room Corporation flats that help to bring some brightness and cleanliness into their lives. But countless hundreds still live in one-room tenements, in basements, in the most rack-rented misery. On every street in the slums are countless children playing and running through the traffic.[2]

There follows a careful catalogue of such children's plight: cramped, damp accommodation; rampant unemployment; poor nourishment and illness; overcrowded classrooms; early school leaving; poorly-paid unskilled work; the attractions of petty crime, etc. A boys' club might ameliorate such hardships:

2. *Boys: A Plan to Help Them,* The Belvedere Newsboys Club, Dublin, 1948, p. 5.

In short, these boys need help, they need to be protected from the evils that everywhere surround them. They need woven into their lives a little human kindness and warmth and joy; and a great deal of human love. These things a club that cares for the boys of the Dublin slums must set before itself to accomplish.[3]

The relationship between club leader – often referred to as 'helper' – and the club members was regarded as central to a successful club. It was a bridge 'across the great gulf of class, environment, age that exits between the two groups'. The quality of personal contact is highlighted and 'nothing – premises, income, facilities of every imaginable kind – can take its place'.[4]

Suggested activities for a club might include swimming, athletics, football, boxing, plays, arts and crafts, billiards, library, draughts and chess. The value of getting to know club members by visiting their homes is emphasised. An annual camp away from the city is proposed.

Suggestions about club premises also give us a flavour of the practical concerns of the times. As well as a games room '... a fire, in winter at least, to sit around and dry wet clothes' and a 'room with water laid on and some means of preparing teas...'. Furthermore, 'every club can provide a washing place for the boys and should insist on a minimum of personal cleanliness.'[5]

A chaplain or spiritual director was viewed as an integral part of the club and ending each club-night with simple prayers was normal. The pamphlet also recognises that club members sometimes get into trouble with the police and that the club should liaise on their behalf with the Gardaí and with probation officers. Referring club members towards appropriate medical

---

3. Ibid. p. 7.

4. Ibid. p. 8.

5. Ibid. p. 11.

services and helping with finding suitable employment are also proposed. Finally, suggestions for complementing formal schooling are wide ranging, from literacy classes, to leatherwork, metalwork, singing and acting.

Noel was attracted to and inspired by this vision of a practical response to poverty. His copy of that pamphlet is well worn. A checklist of a 'helper's attitude' enabled him to focus on the qualities he aspired to as a club leader.

1.  He should be patient, remembering that he, too, was once a boy. He should never condemn a boy as a liar for one lie, or as a thief for petty pilfering. He should remember that the boy's character is not yet formed.
2.  He should not judge the boy too rigidly by his own standards.
3.  He should never patronise; to do so is to antagonise.
4.  He should never be sarcastic; it is cheap and it hurts.
5.  He is an attentive listener who is interested in the boy because he wants to be, not because he has to be.
6.  He should *never* frighten, threaten or strike a boy. He may use one weapon, kindness.
7.  He should *never* give, or worse still, lend the boy money. If he really needs help, refer him to the boys' director.
8.  He should be scrupulous about his conduct and demeanour in the club before the boys.
9.  He must never fail in any promise he may make to the boy, whom he is teaching to follow his example in relations with God and man.
10. He must practise prayer, patience, perseverance, punctuality; these are the characteristics necessary in the successful helper.[6]

While paternalistic and gender specific in tone – reflecting

---

6.  Ibid. p. 17.

the times – many values that inform good practice for those working with young people today are evident. This perspective is also relevant in the wake of the Ryan Report and current child protection concerns, warning youth leaders as people in positions of power against abusing it.

Noel personified many of the positive qualities outlined in that ideal of the youth leader. Friends and co-workers invariably describe him as kind, warm, empathic, non-judgemental, a good listener and role model. Such values underpinned the work of St Vincent's club from its foundations. However, while the club expanded, Noel became restless at work and felt a change was needed.

## A new job

While Noel devoted his spare time primarily to St Vincent's club, brother Seán became deeply involved with the Inchicore branch of Conradh na Gaeilge. This interest in Irish language and culture led Seán to apply, successfully, for a job in Gaeltarra Éireann. In 1959, he began working in the Fenian Street offices of this new semi-state body that had been established in 1957 to promote industrial development in the Gaeltacht regions.[7] Noel saw how much Seán enjoyed his new job. When the next vacancies were advertised, Noel applied. He was also successful. The twins were back working together again.

Gaeltarra Éireann Aran sweaters were popular at home and abroad. Musicians like The Clancy Brothers and Tommy Makem adopted them like a uniform, adding to their glamour. Noel's job in the knitwear division involved dealing with accounts and insurance as well as monitoring production, plant and machinery.

He was good at the work and wasn't slow in suggesting improvements to his immediate boss, Mr Czekanski.

---

7. In 1980 Gaeltarra Éireann was replaced by Údarás na Gaeltachta.

The main production facility was in Tourmakeady, Co. Mayo. It was suggested to Noel that he should relocate to the west of Ireland. Not too keen on the idea, he travelled to Tourmakeady, spent a few days there, returned and politely, but firmly, declined the invitation. Noel, the city boy, knew his heart was in Dublin.

# Chapter 6
## Deeper into Youth Work

The boys' club continued to thrive, not least because of Noel's driving energy. However, he didn't completely neglect other interests. As secretary of the Inchicore branch of Conradh na Gaeilge, he was a dynamic force promoting Irish language and culture locally. For example, the twenty-one year old organised a symposium in Inchicore in 1959 where speakers included the then Supreme Court judge and future President of Ireland, Cearbhall Ó Dálaigh and the well-known 'Rosary priest', Fr Gabriel Harty. In the early 1960s, along with brother Seán and Eamonn O Muirí, Noel organised the annual Inchicore Feis and facilitated the first National Tailteann Irish Dancing Championships.

However, St Vincent's held centre stage. One sign of the thriving boys' club is evident in an *Evening Press* report of the opening of its new premises:

> Inchicore was *en fête* for the opening of the St Vincent's Boys' Club new headquarters at Keogh Square. Flags and bunting decorated approaches to the square, as hundreds of residents assembled for the blessing of the premises by Very Rev. T. F. Meleady, PP.

The report is accompanied by six photographs including one of joint club secretaries Noel Clear and Jerry O'Sullivan.

Football was an early success, remembers Jerry. He recalls starting with fifteen boys from the Square as a team of under sixteens, training two nights a week in the local CIE club grounds. Interest grew, particularly among the boys' parents, as talent and commitment were rewarded. 'Within three years of starting the club, we had six teams playing in various leagues every week,' he recalls.

## Dancing girls

Much schooling and other activities for children at that time tended to be segregated according to gender. Noel's brother Seán, along with Eamonn O Muirí, set up a club for girls, St Brigid's. Irish dancing was very popular; excursions to feiseanna in Kilkenny and Ballyshannon brought prizes, as well as glimpses of countryside that many children in Inchicore rarely saw. The girls' club also offered classes in practical skills such as dressmaking and knitting and organised fashion shows.

## Holidays away from the Square

St Vincent's club summer holidays became legendary. Even today grown men and women retell, with great warmth, incidents from those adventures. The first holiday, in 1961, was to Clonakilty, Jerry O'Sullivan's home town. Jerry, Noel and Seán accompanied forty boys. Father Joseph Sheehan CSSp, a recently ordained missionary about to travel to Nigeria, acted as chaplain to the group. A solicitor, Dr Liam Collins, gave the group a house in which to stay for a fortnight. As word of the initiative spread, other local people chipped in with practical support. Those who remember that holiday still recall fun on Inchydoney beach and Ricky Nelson singing 'Hello Mary Lou' on the jukebox.

Club holidays worked at a number of levels. The break from routine, the different surroundings and a busy schedule of activities engaged everyone's interest, imagination and energy. For city children, a trip to the countryside opened up a different world and provided some very down-to-earth lessons. For one week at least, a somewhat ideal world was created: familiar faces in unfamiliar settings provided both security and novelty; organised games and other activities heightened the fun and laughter; regular wholesome food, night-time singsongs and storytelling added to intensely busy days. For the children's harried parents, one less mouth to feed was a welcome development, especially when they knew their children were safe and secure with the St Vincent's club leaders. For the youth leaders, the relentless encounter with highly energetic children was both tiring and uplifting; importantly, bonds were formed between young people and leaders that developed trust which extended well beyond the holiday.

'These trips were fantastic,' remembers Jerry. His recollections of that first club holiday remain vivid. 'My parents had a farm near the town. The fascination of the boys with the cattle in the fields, how to milk a cow, feed a calf and so much more transformed the holiday into something extraordinary. Even though short, the holiday was the highlight of the year.' Jerry subsequently wrote to the *Southern Star* newspaper thanking every resident of that hospitable town for the warm welcome they extended to the Inchicore boys.

For Noel, that Clonakilty holiday was a pivotal event. He later wrote that, 'Having charge of forty boys for a week, so far from home, is not easy, but we have no regrets or complaints.' He was learning youth leadership skills in a very practical way. For the rest of his life he was a convincing advocate for the multiple benefits of well-organised holidays for young people in difficult circumstances.

## Up in court

From time to time, some club members got into trouble with the law, for stealing or being rowdy, and appeared in court. Noel and Jerry became aware of the difficulties these young people faced with the criminal justice system. In the 1950s, there was no state-assisted legal aid (except in cases where the charge carried the death penalty). Frequently no one spoke up on behalf of the accused youngsters. The experience of children in Keogh Square who had spent time in industrial schools or reformatories such as Upton, Letterfrack, Daingean, Marlborough House or St Patrick's Institution taught the club leaders that such institutions were of questionable value, even counter-productive; some children returned more finely schooled in the ways of lawbreaking. Noel and Jerry began appearing in the courts, speaking on behalf of club members, explaining family contexts and outlining the club's efforts to secure employment and discourage housebreaking and robbery. Jerry remembers some judges congratulating them for their interest in young lawbreakers. Sometimes the boys were returned to the club leaders' care, avoiding custodial sentences.

Noel took this aspect of youth work seriously, often juggling time off work in Gaeltarra Éireann to get to court. Jerry recalls an incident when forty thousand cigarettes were stolen from a shop in Inchicore:

Suspicion fell immediately on the people of Keogh Square. A few nights later a lad came to the club, all upset and worried. Apparently, he had been involved in the robbery. He pleaded with Noel and myself to stay in the club 'till after midnight when he promised he would return with a friend. We stayed and he and his friend arrived a few hours later presenting us with the cartons of cigarettes that they had stolen. There we stood, Noel and myself, surrounded by cigarettes. Not only did neither of us smoke, but what should we do? We worried that the Gardaí might arrive and think we had been protecting the haul for the robbers or for ourselves. Next morning, we went to Kilmainham station. We told our story. The police believed us. But they also wanted those responsible to come to the station too. This was not easy to achieve. But eventually the two boys came. The final result was an admonition from the police and the return to our care of the two involved.

## Practical leadership

The St Vincent's club leaders focused on the practical. Noel was becoming a one-person employment agency, building contacts with employers and placing young people in jobs when positions were scarce and wages meagre. An extract from *The Link*, September 1962 indicates some of the educational and job realities five years before the introduction of 'free' secondary education.

### Boys Leaving School – A Note for Parents

At this time of year several parents are faced with a big decision. A son of theirs has reached fourteen years. Will they put him out to work, or possibly send him off to technical school? At present there are less than a half-dozen boys from the area attending day tech. This is unfortunate for it can be said that boys without some tech training are unsuitable for most kinds of employment. All the trades are closed to them. An example of this is that at present we have two offers of employment from one of Dublin's best-known companies. They want trainees – jobs that would mean a safe future for any boy. But a condition of employment is two years at tech. Unfortunately for us we can offer nobody.

Parents, if you have sons nearing school leaving age, call to the school and discuss with the headmaster your son's ability, interest etc. He will advise you. Possibly you might start him into night tech, if it is essential for the boy to work by day to help the family finances. Don't take the selfish attitude of getting your son earning money at all costs. An extra two years at school can well mean a difference between security and want for the rest of his life.

**Not just a boys' club**

By 1963 St Vincent's was well established. The senior soccer team was in the AUL[1], playing home matches at Red Cow, Clondalkin. Drama activities, under Finbar Howard's direction, were thriving as were cycling trips, swimming in Tara Street baths, visits to museums and art galleries.

*The Link* was becoming a popular publication. Noel and Jerry were busy campaigning for employment possibilities for club members. While sport and drama activities might be described as 'developmental', others were once-off special events designed to bring spark and excitement. For example, in 1962 the club sought financial support from local traders for a Christmas party for two hundred and fifty boys. One can imagine the kind of audience these youngsters made after feasting on crisps, biscuits and cakes, washed down with fizzy lemonade, as they sat down on the floor to watch *Sons of the Musketeers*. In those days, films and projectors had to be hired, windows darkened and reel changes could take time as young audiences got even more impatient!

**Family matters**

While primarily focused on the children, the St Vincent's club leaders inevitably became involved with parents. For some in the Square, the battle against hunger, loneliness and squalor was too much. Alcohol offered the promise of escape. There were

1. Athletic Union League

suicides. In those early days, club leaders, particularly Noel and Jerry, began to visit homes and, as Jerry puts it, 'try to reason with the parents.' While some doors were shut firmly in their faces, others were more welcoming because they knew how much their children benefitted from the club.

The realisation that the children could not be seen in isolation from their families, led to wider provision of services by St Vincent's. Saturday night dances for young people were followed by events on Sunday nights for parents and other adults. Bingo offered a further opportunity for neighbours to come together in a context other than the public house. From very early days, the inclination to be more than a boys' club, to reach out to the rest of the community, was a strong strand in Noel's thinking. The club leaders initiated a parents' committee which later became the first tenants' association in Inchicore.

Looking back across the decades, Jerry O'Sullivan still maintains a strong sense of Noel's presence. 'Basically, life and ideals have not changed,' he contends. 'We still want to live in a better world. We want to see an end to the scourge of alcoholism, drugs, poverty and so much that offends the face of the loving God that gave us this marvellous world with plenty of everything we need, beauty and wealth beyond our imagination. We are a people called to love, to live in the presence of our Creator, to be His friend in the building of a beautiful world, full of everything imaginable, our home and our eternity. Noel has reached that eternity and will live forever in the beatific vision of our Blessed Lord and His Loving Mother.' Jerry speaks for many, many people when he says, 'Thanks, Noel, for all you gave us and all you taught us by example in your extraordinary life. We all miss you but we also know that, in our lives, you live forever.'

# Chapter 7
# Rooted in the Community

The arrival of a national television station in the early 1960s heralded many changes in Irish life. Dancers from St Brigid's Girls Club, Inchicore first performed on the programme *Tír na nÓg* in August 1962, receiving a £5 fee. Later they featured on the popular *Seoirse agus Beartlaí*.

Rooted in the community, Noel delighted in achievements by Inchicore people. He often reminded friends and others how The Bachelors – Declan and Con Cluskey from Tyrconnell Park and John Stokes from Crumlin – climbed high in the UK charts in the 1960s with songs such as 'I Believe', 'Diane', 'Ramona', 'Whispering' and 'Charmaine'.

Noel reminded readers of *The Link* of other local musicians worth celebrating. Derek and Brian Warfield of the Wolfe Tones were from Bluebell. John and Brian Woodfull from Tyrconnell Road played in The Casino Showband and later The Indians. Another Woodfull brother was in the Jim Farley Showband. There were also Inchicore musicians in The Hillbillies, The Radio Showband, The Jolly Tinkers, The Quare Fellas and The Bye-Laws. Noel took great heart from any Inchicore-person-makes-good story, whether in the arts, politics, sport or community service. In 1980, when RTÉ screened one of its best ever dramas, *Strumpet City*,[1] Noel was particularly delighted with local actor Bryan Murray's performance as Fitz, the unemployed worker who ends up in the trenches.

## A Youth Week

The programme of the 1963 Inchicore Youth Week, held between 8 and 15 September, gives a flavour of youth work and the times. The week's events opened with solemn High Mass in St Michael's Church and included sports, an arts and crafts exhibition; Irish music, dancing and singing; soccer matches in Richmond Park; cookery, fashion and table tennis competitions; a seminar for youth leaders and a prizegiving concert. The impressive programme includes advertising from thirty local businesses. A message from Monsignor Cecil J. Barrett of the Youth Welfare Section of the Catholic Social Welfare Bureau states:

> The youth club today must play an important role in the integration of our youth into adult society. Formerly, it could be contented to supply for the spiritual, educational and economic deficiencies in the homes of the underprivileged children. Today, it must broaden its scope to provide healthy outlets for the more affluent youth whose increased pocket money and leisure time expose them to the danger of being exploited. As an ally of the Church, the family and the school, the youth club provides on behalf of the community a sympathetic reception for young people in their quest for maturity and a reliable cushion for their entry into adulthood.

---

1. James Plunkett's epic novel *Strumpet City* captures the lives of ordinary Dubliners caught up in the struggles to survive in the difficult years at the start of the twentieth century. Hugh Leonard adapted the book for TV. In 2013, Dublin City chose the book as its 'One City One Book' book of the year, marking the centenary of the 1913 Lockout.

Two pages later the Minister for Justice writes:

I do not think that it is necessary for me to emphasise how important the success of the youth movement is in our community. Most people are now aware of the aims of the movement, of the unselfish efforts of those many men and women, young and old, lay and clerical, who have devoted and continue to devote themselves to this work and of the excellent results which have been achieved by them.

Their efforts have earned the goodwill of the community. What is needed now, however, is a means of converting that goodwill into practical support, not only by way of material assistance but also by the active participation in organised youth activities by a great many people in every area. A programme such as the Inchicore Youth Week, addressed not only to the parish clubs but to the whole parish, should have very beneficial results in this regard and I have very great pleasure in wishing it every possible success.

This message is signed 'Charles J. Haughey'.

A newspaper report of youth week events notes that the well-known Liffey swimmer Chalkie White was a surprise guest. Children were asked to guess his identity. The prize-winner who knew most about the legendary swimmer was a Gabriel Mitchell of Ring Street. The latter went on to represent Dublin South West in Dáil Éireann and Dublin in the European Parliament. He also served as Lord Mayor of Dublin in 1993.

The young people of Keogh Square also took part in some memorable performances of Seán O'Casey's plays. For many, the playwright's themes and characters were not merely historical; it was as if Joxer Daly, Jack Boyle and Bessie Burgess were local residents. As well as capturing the tensions, frustrations and humour in O'Casey's work, drama teacher Finbar Howard also ensured the well-crafted lines were enunciated clearly and in wonderfully authentic accents.

## Winds of Change

For as long as Noel could remember, the Pope in Rome, the head of the Church, was Pope Pius XII, Eugenio Pacelli. When he died, in October 1958, there was some mild surprise when the cardinals elected a seventy-seven year old to succeed him. Pope John XXIII, Angelo Guiseppe Roncalli, was regarded as an interim appointment, a 'stop gap' pope. But, as one commentator has written:

> Yet in a mere four-and-a-half-years Pope John XXIII transformed the Roman Catholic Church and gave a new image to the papacy. He called the Second Vatican Council and gave it a vision for the future. People saw in him the Good Shepherd of the Gospels. When he died on 3 June 1963 the whole world mourned. No pope had been so loved.[2]

Pope John's 1961 encyclical letter *Mater et Magistra* sparked great interest in Noel and others. The Pope set out a vision of the Church as mother and teacher, concerned with the practical problems facing humanity such as hunger and poverty. He emphasised the responsibilities of owners of property and wealth, as well as the rights of workers. The Pope stressed that social, political and economic decisions and policies should be directed towards 'the common good'.

---

2. P. Hebblethwaite, *John XXIII: Pope of the Council*, London: Geoffrey Chapman, 1984.

These fresh developments in the Church triggered many thoughts in Noel's head. A recurring question was: should he offer himself for the priesthood? He was then in his mid-twenties. While aware that most entered the seminary immediately after school, his first-cousin Joe Kelly, was a living example of a 'late vocation'.

The scale of urban poverty that he had glimpsed on visits to Great Britain led him to consider an English diocese. Noel wrote to the seminary in Thurles, Co. Tipperary and received an encouraging reply. Eventually, he applied to the Dublin Diocesan Seminary. A reference dated 9 July 1963 and written by Thomas Meleady PP was succinct, with few frills. It stated:

Mr Noel Clear of number fifty Tyrconnell Road, Inchicore belongs to a most respectable family. He is a very good, intelligent, pious young man, of excellent character and I have pleasure in recommending him as a suitable candidate to study for the priesthood.

And so, in September 1963, Noel, armed with the black clerical uniform of the seminarian, entered the gates of Clonliffe College in Drumcondra on the north side of the city. Once inside, Noel, who had agonised for a long time over his decision, who had enjoyed farewell parties, quickly decided that this was not the life for him. He left the following morning! Noel was so quick in making his decision, some of his fellow seminarians never set eyes on him. 'I remember on the second day hearing something about a bloke who had left already but, to be honest, we were all so caught up in our own decisions, that it didn't register that much at the time,' recalls one of the 1963 cohort.

Coincidentally, Noel's parents happened to be attending a funeral in Glasnevin on the day he departed Clonliffe. Noel had given his Morris Minor to his father and knew they would be returning through Drumcondra. 'I was in the back of the car and I remember shouting, "Look, there's Noel,"' recalls Tony. Jack and Úna, while surprised, were delighted to pick him up and bring him home to Inchicore.

Years afterwards, Noel often said that entering the seminary was something he felt he had to do at the time.[3] He had no regrets about his decision to go into Clonliffe, or to leave. Seán thinks that the whole institutional nature of Clonliffe turned him off. 'Maybe he saw the clerical way as putting a barrier between himself and people,' he suggests.

Auxiliary Bishop of Dublin, Eamonn Walsh, got to know Noel when working as a chaplain in St Patrick's Institution when Noel was probation and welfare officer there. He recalls: 'I have many great memories of Noel beginning with his "bed and breakfast" stay at Clonliffe. After the first night he left his soutane at the front gate having realised that priesthood was not his calling. *Is fearr rith maith na droch seasamh.'*[4] Bishop Eamonn continues:

Noel, like many others, decided to try Clonliffe because he wanted to do good. The good he was called to do he discerned quickly was in a different way to priesthood. Some people present themselves as being people for people but Noel Clear was the real deal, he was what it said on the tin. It was a blessing for Ireland that he chose the path he did and to have his goodness live on in his family and so many lives that he touched for the better.

---

3. John O'Brien, now a Spiritan missionary in Pakistan, captures the Clonliffe episode in a poem 'One Night Stand', in his collection *On the Edge of Words*, Grangecon Press, 2017.

4. Literally 'a good run is better than a bad stand' is sometimes interpreted as 'It is better to turn and run away and live to fight another day' or even 'Discretion is the better part of valour.' It also can refer to someone deciding the night before a wedding to run away from it.

Whatever the reasons for Noel's entry to and departure from Clonliffe College, he quickly moved on to the next stage of his life.

# Chapter 8
## Working for Justice

'That's the job for me,' declared Noel when he saw the newspaper advertisement. The Department of Justice was expanding its welfare service. Having decided that the ordained priesthood was not for him, Noel returned to work in Gaeltarra Éireann but was still restless. The possibility of working full-time for the welfare of young lawbreakers was attractive. Despite lacking formal qualifications for the job, he had noted the wording in the advertisement: 'exceptional personal qualities and exceptional experience in an appropriate field of social work.'[1] Noel applied and was called for interview. His future employers obviously recognised the value of his youth work activities, his organisational ability and advocacy work with marginalised young people. They offered Noel the job. He accepted enthusiastically.

Noel began work sharing an office in Ormond Quay with fellow probation and welfare officers Kay Kinsella, John Ryan, Martin Tansey and Mary Dooley. He was delighted to be paid an annual salary of £600 for work he was growing to love. Much of his first two years were spent in the Children's Court, assessing young people's situations for district justices. These experiences

---

1. Circular letter 13.59.63 sets out some of the conditions of service.

provided fresh insights into familiar patterns: the vast majority of those in trouble with the law had not performed well at school, were from families that had few resources and lived in areas with high concentrations of convicted lawbreakers. Some addresses were high predictors of future imprisonment.

## Inheritance

The probation service in Britain and Ireland was shaped by the 1907 Probation of Offenders Act where probation officers' duties were defined as:

> To visit or receive reports from the probationer, to see that he observes the conditions of the order, to report to the Court on his behaviour, and to advise and befriend him, and, where necessary, to try to find him employment.[2]

Following independence in 1922, the probation service in Ireland was run by a very small number of probation officers: one in 1926, four in 1936.[3] In 1937 there were two hundred and eighty-nine people under supervision, one hundred and fifty-seven of them under eighteen years of age. For much of the early years of the state, the work of the employed probation officers was supplemented by the voluntary efforts of members of recognised organisations such as the Legion of Mary, the Society of St Vincent de Paul, the Salvation Army and the Quaker Community.

In his account of the development of the Irish probation service, McNally states:

---

2. The gendered nature of the language in this piece of legislation also reveals the thinking at the time about who was likely to be on probation or indeed, a probation officer.

3. McNally, 'Probation in Ireland: A Brief History of the Early Years' in *Irish Probation Journal*, Vol 4, No.1 September, 2007, p. 11.

From the early 1940s, there was a strengthening explicit preference in government for the engagement of voluntary denominational organisations in the provision of probation supervision and related services rather than the development of a full-time state service.[4]

In the Children's Court, Noel observed the traffic of children as young as seven years of age in and out of the legal system. There he got to know the children's parents, seeing them struggle as, frequently, they lacked sufficient money to feed their families. Mothers confided in Noel that the heartbreak of seeing a son sentenced to Daingean or Letterfrack was sometimes tempered by the realisation that it meant one less mouth to feed.

## St Patrick's

In 1966 Noel was appointed as welfare officer to St Patrick's Institution, adjacent to Mountjoy Jail, where sixteen to eighteen-year-old males served time.[5] His role was defined as being 'responsible for advising ordinary prisoners on personal and domestic problems, for helping them to secure employment and for giving of after-discharge counsel and guidance'.[6] His primary concern was the welfare of those serving their sentences and about to be released. Noel also built good relationships with prison staff, psychiatrists, psychologists and others, as well

---

4. McNally (2007) p. 13.

5. St Patrick's Institution was formally closed on 7 April 2017.

6. McNally (2007, p. 13) notes that Minister for Justice, Charles Haughey, at the Law Students Debating Society of Ireland in February 1964, announced the appointment of two prison welfare officers (Martin Tansey and Noel Clear) to be 'responsible for advising ordinary prisoners on personal and domestic problems, for helping them to secure employment and for giving of after-discharge counsel and guidance' (quoted in *The Spirit of the Nation: The Speeches and Statements of Charles J. Haughey (1957–1986)*, Edited by M. Mansergh, Cork: Mercier Press. p. 40.

as potential employers. Furthermore, he maintained contact with the young inmates' families and organised rehabilitation programmes within the prison.

Noel's warm relationships with many who served time is echoed in a recurring story that his son Alan recalls from his childhood. They would be walking in the street together, father and son, when a man – nearly always a man – came up to Noel. A conversation, usually with some laughter, followed. Invariably, when the conversation ended Alan would ask, 'Who is that, Da?' or 'How do you know him?' Noel's typical response was, 'When he was young he was in a bit of trouble, ended up in prison. Ah, he was a nice young lad.' Alan's recollections resonate with the memories of many of Noel's colleagues who remember his positive disposition to everyone who crossed his path.

According to Tom Gilmore, a friend and colleague of Noel's, becoming the first probation and welfare officer in St Patrick's Institution for young offenders was very challenging. 'You can imagine, as with many organisations, those prison officers working on the inside didn't welcome those they saw as "civilians" sticking their noses into their business. Noel handled the situation brilliantly,' says Tom. 'He knew how to apply his considerable people skills, how to work with prisoners, prison officers, governors, families and so on.'

As a probation and welfare officer, Noel built on his experience as a volunteer youth worker. Then – as now – a brush with the law did little to enhance one's employability. Noel cultivated trust among employers, especially in the hotel and construction industries. He valued those willing to offer his clients a fresh start, who were discreet and knew that their customers need not worry about the record of those who peeled the potatoes in the kitchen or dug the trenches on a building site. Experience had also taught Noel that many a teenage tearaway settled down in his early twenties.

## Emigrants

Noel discovered, with resonances of Keogh Square, that the boat to England offered former inmates the attraction of a fresh start, often without having to explain a criminal record. Many were poorly equipped for life in London or other cities and this increased the urgency Noel and his colleagues felt to find them work and accommodation at home. He also established contacts with staff in British prisons and various welfare organisations.

In 1966, participation in a Council of Europe study visit to probation and welfare services in England enabled Noel to examine some British prisons, borstals, detention centres and probation hostels. As often happens with such educational trips, it became an important reference point, encouraging him to imagine how Irish services might be improved.

Kay Kinsella joined the probation and welfare service in the late 1960s. 'Although I was an experienced social worker, I had not worked close to the prisons and Noel was always there to guide me when I had to enter uncharted waters! I found him to be a very good friend to approach for guidance.' Later, when both worked together in developing the service and in the provision of staff training, Kay recalled, 'I came to appreciate his teamwork, kindness and good humour. No matter what difficulties we had to face in the prison or court work or planning and training for new staff, Noel had great energy and was always deeply interested in the projects that were being developed.'

Noel's kindness and good humour were strong assets, Kay recalled. 'I got a deep sense of his great care for his clients and his co-workers, professional and otherwise,' she said. 'I remember he had a wide range of contacts in voluntary organisations. He related so well to people, never criticising or blaming.'

Kay also recalled how Noel was always ready to help colleagues with personal difficulties; whenever he saw a need to be fulfilled, he sought a solution. He was very good at rallying other staff to help, discreetly of course. 'Noel seemed to be able to make light of problems with a toss of his head and a big smile!' added Kay.

Tom Gilmore's views echo Kay's. 'Noel was always very determined but had a great knack of not appearing to threaten anyone. He struggled, as many of us did, with bureaucracy. His human instincts were to be sceptical of rules and what he saw as unnecessary red tape. He was very human, excellent at dealing with staff who had any issues. As a boss, he was very supportive, encouraging, trusting, not into micro-management, allowing you get on with working with the offenders,' says Tom.

Tom saw the rapid expansion of the probation and welfare service up close. 'Seven or eight new people were recruited in May 1971 and ten or twelve of us in November of that year. That's when I joined. It grew from a service of five or six to nearly thirty in a short space of time. Morale was very good because we all saw ourselves in a sort of crusading role; we were pioneering lots of things. It was an exciting time,' he recalls.

### Young lawbreakers – a Christian view

Paul Cavadino, who worked with the National Association for the Care and Resettlement of Offenders (NACRO) in Britain, has written about how Christians might regard convicted lawbreakers.

I am very interested in Christian principles, and particularly Catholic social teachings, as they apply to offenders. The Gospels are about seeking out lost sheep and celebrating the return of the Prodigal Son. Jesus spent his time with prostitutes and sinners and was castigated for it by the establishment. He spent his last night as a remand prisoner and his last act was to forgive a fellow condemned criminal. When he gave us a shortlist of how to be saved it included visiting prisoners.

If society is to be consistent with Christian principles then rehabilitation must be at the heart of the system. Society has a right to punish people who have transgressed against others or society itself and has a duty to protect the weak.

It's particularly offensive to justice that many prisoners with a severe mental illness are being held in prisons rather than in hospitals – secure ones where necessary – or in other health or social-care settings.[7]

Noel shared much of Cavadino's perspective. While initially happy to be employed by the State to work with those in trouble with the law, Noel was never comfortable with the harsh realities of the juvenile justice system. He worked 'from the inside' to try to humanise it. Other probation and welfare officers also grappled with the dilemma of being part of the system and wanting to improve it.

---

7. 'In Defence of Offenders', *The Tablet*, 1 November 2008, p. 14–15.

# Chapter 9
## Tensions at St Vincent's

As Noel settled into his day job in the probation and welfare service, St Vincent's club continued to dominate his evenings and weekends. When, in 1963, Jerry O'Sullivan left Ireland for South America as a Legion of Mary envoy, Noel became the single leader of the venture. He missed his friend and they corresponded regularly, often discussing their hopes and fears for the club they had founded.

A niggling tension developed from a view that a Legion of Mary volunteer should give two hours per week to Legion work. Noel believed that if the club was to thrive, much more time was needed. This became a matter of disagreement between himself and the parish priest, Fr Meleady. In an undated letter from that period Noel wrote, in some frustration, that the praesidium had reduced the number of club nights to three; the over-age section had been disbanded and there was no longer a football team. This, he argued, was short-changing the young people of the area. The letter contended that 'there is a complete difference between the proper control of a youth club and the control of a praesidium doing perhaps house-to-house visitation ... perhaps it might be said that the Legion system does not lend itself to the proper control of a youth club.'

Tensions relating to St Brigid's Girls' Club that Noel's brother Seán had founded also surfaced. The parish priest, citing the archbishop, maintained that it was inappropriate for a man to be conducting a club for girls. Initially irritated, Seán consulted his friend Eamonn Ó Muirí. Eamonn proposed that a neighbour, Jean Clune, might assist in running the dancing classes and satisfy the gender issue. The suggestion was spectacularly successful. Not only did Jean become a very good Irish dancing teacher, Seán and herself started going out together and the couple married in 1967.

Meanwhile, Noel's enthusiasm for developing St Vincent's showed no sign of waning. He imagined how a dedicated premises might enhance the project. However, Legion of Mary authorities were displeased that he appeared to be acting independently. The President of the Benedicta Curia in North Frederick Street, somewhat exasperated, wrote to Noel in May 1964:

Once again, in exercise of my duties and responsibilities as Curia President, I am forced to write to you. I find it very difficult to reconcile your many protestations of loyalty to the Legion of Mary with your action of submitting far-reaching proposals regarding St Vincent's Boys' Club to an outside body without even submitting them to the praesidium.

In the past I spoke to you of the danger of independent action and the vital necessity of trying to accept, not only willingly, but cheerfully, the decisions of those in authority, no matter how hard, both clerical and lay.

To say the least, your action was ill-advised and ill-timed especially in view of the Curia's intention to appoint a new president to your praesidium.

It appears to me that you must decide, without yea or nay, whether you wish to help the Church and serve Our Lady within the ranks of the Legion of Mary or whether you consider you can do more for the Mystical Body of Christ by carrying on the apostolate in another sphere or organisation.

Should you decide to remain in the Legion, you have no alternative but to live your Promise –'Confident that Thou will so receive me – and use me – and turn my weakness into strength this day, I take my place in the ranks of the Legion, and I venture to promise a faithful service. I will submit fully to its discipline, which binds me to my comrades and shapes us as an Army, and keeps our line as on we march with Mary[1]'.

Should you decide that your work for the Church could be better performed outside our ranks, then I hope and pray that we will be able to co-operate for the greater glory of God and the salvation of souls.

May Our Lady, Queen and Mother, whose Feast we celebrate on Sunday, intercede with the Most Holy Spirit so that He may help you to seek, know, accept and follow God's Holy Will in your decision.

This letter caused Noel great distress. His loyalty to the Legion clashed with his inclination to abandon it. He continued to negotiate with the Legion, maintaining that, acting at all times in the interests of the youth of Keogh Square, he was implementing the will of God. He sought advice from Jerry in Venezuela. Legion envoy Jerry was in no doubt about Noel's integrity and commitment to the people in the Square and believed the matter could be resolved.

Noel's persistence prompted a follow-up letter later that summer from the head office, effectively seeking Noel's resignation. It stated:

---

1. The full text of the Legion promise (2005 version) can be found in the Legion of Mary Handbook *Legio Mariae* at https://is.gd/legion2005

... arising from Curia discussion of the annual report of your praesidium, and further to recent discussions at Curia and with yourself, I have been directed by the Curia to put the following two questions to you:

(a) Are you prepared to live up to your Legion promise?

(b) Are you prepared to loyally accept the Legion discipline and accept decisions of and rulings of your praesidium?

Should you be unable for any reason to give an unqualified 'yes' to both these questions, then I have been directed to request your resignation. If you are unable to give an unqualified 'yes' to the questions and refuse to offer your resignation, I have no alternative but to suspend you from Legion membership for an indefinite period.

The letter includes details of how to contact the president by phone. Stubbornly, Noel didn't resign. He continued to be a strong force in running St Vincent's club and in expanding the 1964 Inchicore Youth Week. His local praesidium was also responsible for the erection of a shrine to Our Lady in Keogh Square which Fr Meleady blessed on 19 July. Fortunately, an alternative strategy began to emerge for Noel.

## New directions

Father Peter Lemass was a curate based in St Michael's parish. A member of the Radharc television team that produced many ground-breaking documentaries on social and religious issues, his distinctive voice and commentary still resonate clearly whenever those old films pop up on television. Noel discussed the Legion of Mary situation with the priest. An intriguing question, and possible solution, presented itself from their discussions: why not run the club under the auspices of the Society of St Vincent de Paul? This would ensure continuity of service to the young people and enable the adult leaders to remain 'onside' with the Church authorities. The SVP was organised through a series of branches, known as conferences, operating at parish level, which responded, often by giving practical aid, to those needing support. 'Person-to-person' contact was a key feature and visiting homes had expanded in various directions including hospital, prison and orphanage visits, educational and youth work. A thriving network of youth clubs in various Dublin parishes promised a new support structure for the Inchicore club. The more Noel and Peter talked, the more the idea made sense. They also bonded, sharing their concerns about the conditions of those living in Keogh Square. The priest's outspokenness also impressed Noel.

One public expression of his views indicates the priest's disposition. This occurred at the 1967 annual general meeting of the Irish Society for the Prevention of Cruelty to Children (ISPCC) and caused consternation. When Fr Lemass spoke about 'the sub-standard accommodation which the corporation had been closing for twenty years,' he was interrupted by the Fianna Fáil Lord Mayor, Councillor Thomas Stafford. The Lord Mayor said that 'Father Lemass mentioned the corporation and as I am the chairman of that council for housing our people I must take issue with him'. Councillor Stafford added that forty-five to fifty thousand dwellings were their responsibility but they had only twenty-five to thirty social workers. There were many problems, he continued, particularly people not paying rent. They had to be brought to court and ejected from their dwellings as 'this is the law of the land'. He asserted that if the corporation had not a place to put these people they would have to go and live in the park. They must have sub-standard dwellings to house those evicted from corporation houses, noting that there were ten thousand one hundred families on the corporation's housing waiting list.

Undeterred, Fr Lemass asserted that one could expect nothing else but illiteracy and delinquency when people were put to live in what the corporation euphemistically called sub-standard accommodation in an old army barracks of grey granite slabs, unfit for habitation forty years after the British Army moved out. The priest painted a picture where primitive sanitation, erratic water supply, windows as often knocked out, walls like subterranean streams, so damp 'that wallpaper would not stick to them and where landings and hallways were fouled by dogs and others.' He continued, 'Can you expect a father to sit in at night over the living-room fire, where all around him are draughts, noise, damp and the cries of children? He goes to the only warm snug he knows, and where trouble is never far away; Mountjoy is always around the corner especially when you are already a past pupil.' Father Lemass then focused on the children's suffering:

> You can see it in their pinched, pale faces, in their raucous shouts, in gangs that parade the roads at night, in the aimless lounging of the aimless adolescents, in the snotty noses of the young ones, raggy clothes, trousers too long, mouth sticky and black. Yes, you can get free dinners from the Mercy convent nearby, but where is the dignity of the family in this, what does home mean, a damp, cold, draughty granite cell, where the telly disappears on the Friday night if father is short for his pints?

The children, he continued, suffered from lack of schooling, from their physical surroundings and were affected morally and emotionally. The school attendance laws seem to be largely ineffective, he added. He had never seen, in any part of the world to which he had travelled, conditions more degrading, an atmosphere more depressing, or an environment more hopeless that in Keogh Square, Inchicore. There were only a few areas in Dublin in a similar position – Corporation Place, Marshalsea Barracks and Benburb Street[2].

While Fr Lemass's comments generated some newspaper interest, the corporation didn't appear in any rush to abandon Keogh Square or the policy of concentrating families with difficulties in a single location. Furthermore, a telling illustration of how stereotypical views of individuals, groups or communities can develop emerges from an anonymous column in *The Irish Press* in February 1967. The article so infuriated Noel's brother Seán, that he wrote a spirited response. The ill-informed journalist implied that there were no facilities for young people in Keogh Square. Seán outlined the range of opportunities offered by the boys' and girls' clubs, also mentioning the work of the residents association, the Legion of Mary and the St Vincent de Paul. Seán was keenly aware that the work he, Noel and others were doing was supported through modest fundraising and feared that negative publicity would deter supporters. Seán also wanted to refute any implication that the people were not 'respectable'. It's a lively letter worth reading in full.[3]

## Under new management

Encouraged by Fr Lemass's suggestions and support, Noel contacted old friends from the other end of Inchicore where St Joseph's Boys' Club had operated successfully since the mid-1940s. Based on Tyrconnell Road, 'Joey's' had a strong reputation for organising football teams, hikes in the Wicklow mountains, musicals, swimming in the Iveagh and Tara Street Baths, holidays

---

2. *The Irish Times*, 13 October, 1967, 'Strong views at ISPCC meeting, Lord Mayor takes offence.'

3. The full text of the *Irish Press* 'Onlooker' column and Seán's response can be found in Liam O'Meara's 2016 book *Who Remembers Keogh Square?* Inchicore, Dublin: Riposte Books.

to SVP holiday centres in Lonan Murphy House, Co. Kildare and, after that burned down, Kerdiffstown House. The famous St Patrick's Athletic and Ireland soccer player Ginger O'Rourke had begun his playing career with St Joseph's under eleven team. The politician brothers, Jim and Gay Mitchell, were both youth leaders in the club. Soon, the transition from praesidium to conference, from Legion of Mary to SVP auspices, was under way and completed relatively smoothly.

Brendan Kinsella became president of the new SVP conference, named St Patrick's. Brendan Comerford was treasurer. Other leaders from St Joseph's Club who transferred included Colbert Byrne and Gay McGrath. Fresh blood brought fresh ideas and a new energy to St Vincent's. Noel worked well with his new colleagues and he felt the club was in safe hands.

## Social life

One might reasonably ask, was there no social life? Was Noel, now in his late-twenties, totally absorbed by his probation and welfare work and St Vincent's club? Occasionally, Noel and Seán attended the Mansion House ceilidh on a Saturday night, no doubt as identical twins causing confusion among fellow dancers. Noel was not a regular drinker and when he did go to pubs, it was usually to listen to a ballad session. The Abbey Tavern in Howth and the Embankment in Tallaght were popular venues. As far as sport was concerned, Noel was happy to watch teams from the youth club. He occasionally visited Croke Park to see Dublin playing and, more rarely, dropped in to Richmond Park to see local Inchicore League of Ireland side St Patrick's Athletic play. Seán recalls that the dancehall of choice was The Crystal. However, it seemed that, at that stage anyway, Noel was almost too busy to have a regular girlfriend.

Showbands were extremely popular in the 1960s and, like thousands of other young people, Noel was a fan. The Royal Showband, fronted by Brendan Bowyer, was a particular favourite. So was Dickie Rock of the Miami Showband. Noel sometimes travelled well outside Dublin to listen to these bands. He even attended, in June 1967, the opening of a 'teen and twenty boutique' in Pim's of George's Street. This shop was marketed as the place for 'all young Dubliners seeking the latest in fashion fabrics, trends and colours.' Noel came away from Pim's with an autographed picture of a singer he admired and occasionally imitated, Dickie Rock.

Unfortunately, Noel never danced to the Dolphin Showband with whom his brother Tony was the trumpet player for fourteen months. Tony often played three and four nights a week, a demanding schedule on top of his day job in the Gas Company. Tony jokes about Noel, 'He never even asked for my autograph.'

## *Chapter 10*
# The Times They are a Changin'

Chroniclers of the 1960s tend to highlight 1968 as a special year. Riots and strikes in Paris are seen as symbolising a new generation, determined to create a freer society. In April, civil rights leader Martin Luther King was assassinated in Memphis, Tennessee; two months later Senator Robert Kennedy was shot in Los Angeles; George Best won the European Cup, with some help from his Manchester United teammates; in October, a civil rights march in Derry would became a defining moment in the history of social justice in Northern Ireland. For many, including the thirty-year-old Noel, the changing times carried hope and the promise of a better society.

The year 1968 was also an important one in St Vincent's. The change in management to an SVP conference had strengthened the club. That summer two successful week-long holidays took place. Sixty-four teenage boys from the club, accompanied by an energetic team of twelve leaders, descended on the holiday camp in Knockadoon, Co. Cork. These youth leaders and conference members, mainly in their twenties and thirties, had raised £600 since January to fund the event. They were also giving up a week of their annual holidays. Against a relentless soundtrack of 'Young

Girl' by Gary Puckett & The Union Gap and limited sleep they sought to channel the energy of their youthful charges. Secondly, thirty girls from the club spent a week in Aughrim, Co. Wicklow accompanied by five women leaders. That holiday cost £100, also raised by the conference. It is estimated that prices have increased between fifteen and twenty times since 1968.

In 1967, Tom Gilmore, who had known both Noel and Jerry O'Sullivan before becoming a seminarian with the Spiritans (Holy Ghost Fathers), was based in Kimmage Manor, a relatively short bicycle journey from Inchicore. Tom was also studying at University College Dublin, and was among the first cohort of students to grace the new Belfield campus. Tom became an active member of the conference and a voluntary youth leader. Following Tom's initiative, numerous other Spiritan seminarians became involved in St Vincent's activities. Young, energetic and idealistic, they saw engagement with the young people of Keogh Square closely related to the Spiritan mission to 'the poor and most abandoned'. Furthermore, in the excitement that followed the Second Vatican Council, the traditional isolation of seminarians from 'ordinary people' was being challenged, especially by the seminarians themselves. Youth club involvement was a concrete expression of new priorities. Later that year, some of the Kimmage seminarians were instrumental in organising their fellow UCD students into a carol singing group that located itself in Grafton Street. The Singing Scientists entertained the passing Christmas shoppers and rattled their collection boxes for St Vincent's club. That initial venture of 1968 was so successful and enjoyable that fundraising events by the 'Singing Scientists' from Belfield became an established tradition that continues to this day. Noel related well to the young men from Kimmage Manor and was delighted to see additional resources coming into the club.

## The new curate

In the autumn of 1968, the appointment of Fr Brian Power as curate in St Michael's parish was a significant development for Noel and St Vincent's. Brian, a Dubliner, then thirty-eight years old, had spent the previous four years as a university chaplain, based in UCD, Earlsfort Terrace. He was a popular and progressive priest, enthused by Vatican II. He was also a writer. He had conducted a study of the opinions and attitudes of university students on religious and social matters[1]. Brian was also writing short stories and would go on to win a Hennessy Award a few years later. In UCD, he enabled the student society Pax Romana grow in numbers as it became a popular forum for discussing topical issues of the day. John Feeney, a leading figure in UCD's gentle revolution, and John Bruton, later leader of Fine Gael and Taoiseach (1994–1997), were among those who honed their debating skills under Fr Power's guidance.

Not everyone, however, was happy with the dynamic chaplain's approach. Complaints about Fr Power's progressive initiatives found their way to Archbishop John Charles McQuaid. The priest was summoned to the palace in Drumcondra and asked to explain why he had celebrated Mass (in Newman House on St Stephen's Green) without a proper altar-stone. The archbishop was not impressed with the explanation and shortly afterwards Brian Power received a letter telling him he was being transferred. UCD's loss was about to become Inchicore's gain.

In the biography *John Charles McQuaid: Ruler of Catholic Ireland,* John Cooney described this move as 'a humbling demotion for an intellectual and literary man who was highly popular with students'. Cooney continues:

---

1. A detailed account of that survey appeared in 1969 as a supplement to *Reality* magazine, published by the Irish Redemptorists. It can be read at *www.brianpowerswriting.ie*

However, there was a further twist to the story. Just as Power was packing his belongings at the chaplaincy, he received word that the head of the Philosophy Department, Monsignor John Horgan, wanted to see him. 'If you play ball you can remain as chaplain,' Horgan told Power. 'Playing ball' meant undertaking to reform Pax Romana, cut off its funding from the university authorities and pass the grant over to the diocese. Power refused to co-operate on those terms and was duly dispatched to a curacy in Inchicore, while Boland (Fr Paul Boland, head chaplain) was instructed by McQuaid to form a new Pax Romana which would be strictly Catholic in membership, a venture doomed to failure in view of the dissatisfaction felt by the students at the shabby treatment of their assistant chaplain.[2]

Dispatched to Inchicore, one of the first encounters Fr Brian Power had when he arrived was with John Walsh and Jim Guider, two of Noel's fellow youth leaders in St Vincent's. Friends since schooldays, John had recently encouraged Jim to join him as a member of the SVP conference that ran the club. John was always forceful and outspoken. 'I was impressed by how passionately John spoke about the needs of the children in Keogh Square,' Brian Power recalled later. As an SVP conference, they needed a chaplain. It looked like they had found one. 'At first, I think we were all sceptical as to how this guy from Dún Laoghaire and UCD was going to fit into Inchicore, yes, all of us, including Noel,' recalls Jim. It didn't take long for the soft-spoken priest to win the hearts and minds of the conference members and the people of Keogh Square.

---

2. J. Cooney, *John Charles McQuaid, Ruler of Catholic Ireland*, Dublin: O'Brien Press, 1999, p. 389.

Jim recalls an occasion, early in 1969, when Fr Power and himself were passing a cluster of older teenagers, when it dawned on him how well the new curate had settled in. 'There was a lot about black power in the US in the news at the time,' says Jim and when they saw us, they began punching the air, chanting: "Black Power, Brian Power, Father Power". I remember thinking that it was quite a statement of acceptance,' says Jim. Brian became deeply involved in the club, often facilitating and encouraging lengthy discussions about how best to respond to some very needy young people and their families. Noel and Brian[3] worked particularly well together and became great friends.

Mick O'Connell was one of the Kimmage students who volunteered in St Vincent's. He later qualified as a social worker and worked in London in the probation service and with people who abused alcohol and other drugs. The years in the youth club are very special for him. 'I think I learned more in Vincent's than I did on the university course,' he laughs. 'There you were shown how to work with people in a brilliant way. I learned to be straight with people, to be relaxed with people and to be confident with people. I think it stood to me all my life'. As Mick remembers it, 'it wouldn't have been possible without Noel and Brian. They provided the guidance and were kind of pulling the strings in the background'. For Mick, many of the insights gained in Inchicore informed his approach to working with people on the margins of society. 'I saw at first hand that if you encouraged and promoted people who had been in trouble, really gave them a chance, they often responded in surprisingly positive ways'. To illustrate the point Mick describes a club holiday to Garron Tower, Co. Antrim in 1969. 'There were maybe seven of us adult

3. Inchicore features in various guises in Fr Brian Power's subsequent writing, including short stories and poems. Furthermore, 'A Poem for Noel', dedicated to 'Anne Clear, Rory, Alan and Conor' was published in *Lighthouse Blinking* (2006) and can be read at *www.brianpowerswriting.ie*

leaders. Noel was also very trusting of the older club members. He saw them as future leaders even though they might have had scrapes with the law. It worked brilliantly on the bus on the way up when some younger members started singing offensive and sectarian songs. The older lads took to their responsibilities with relish! Throughout the week, during the frantic activities – games, athletics, football matches – you could see these guys developing as leaders, exercising real responsibility. I was always impressed by how respectful Noel was to people, no matter what their background,' says Mick.

## The impact of Vatican II

In terms of changing times and views, Noel was also absorbing the many fresh ideas that were emerging within the Catholic Church in the wake of the Second Vatican Council (1962-1965). The shift in emphasis of the reforming Pope John XXIII from severity and condemnation towards mercy and compassion appealed to Noel. Seeing Protestants as fellow Christians made more sense to him than defining them as people whose beliefs were erroneous. He also liked the changing image of the Church less as a pyramid with the Pope at the apex and the laity at the base to one that was more circular and flat. Regarding the Church as the 'People of God' was seriously liberating. Noel was also aware of a renewed emphasis on scripture, religious liberty, and the role of conscience. Like many Catholics at that time, Noel also found himself questioning and rethinking much of the religious education he had received at school. He wasn't totally convinced that the Council was simply a continuation of what had gone before.

Archbishop McQuaid's perspective on the Council didn't quite resonate. As Fuller remarks:

McQuaid's attitude to changes in the Church was best captured by his remarks addressed to the congregation when he preached at thanksgiving devotions in the Pro-Cathedral on the day he returned from the Council. Referring to the fact that in the previous four years people may 'have been disturbed at times by reports from the Council', he was at pains to lay any such anxieties to rest. He went on: 'You may have been worried by much talk of changes to come. Allow me to reassure you. No change will worry the tranquillity of your Christian lives.' As the years passed, of course, it became obvious to him that profound changes were taking place in Catholicism all around him, despite his efforts to resist them.[4]

The tone of the Council is well captured in the Pastoral Constitution on the Church in the Modern World, *Gaudium et Spes*. This presents the Church – the People of God – as pilgrims on the road of history in solidarity with other human beings, grappling with the many challenges posed by modern life and the need to read what Pope John XXIII called 'the signs of the times'. The Constitution begins: 'The joys and the hopes, griefs and anxieties of the people of this age, especially the poor ... are the joys and hopes, griefs and anxieties of the followers of Christ ... nothing genuinely human fails to raise an echo in our hearts.' Noel warmed to this vision and valued being able to discuss aspects of the changes with Fr Power and fellow conference members.

### Changing family

Amid the many social changes, 1969 brought some personal challenges for Noel. Twin brother Seán and his wife Jean moved

---

4. L. Fuller, *Irish Catholicism Since 1950, The Undoing of a Culture*, Dublin: Gill and Macmillan, 2002, p. 112.

to Galway. This was the biggest separation for the twins in more than three decades and a time of adjustment for Noel.

During the previous two years Noel's mother, Úna, had been in and out of hospital. In November 1969, she was in Dr Steevens' Hospital again, for what turned out to be the final time. Úna died on 13 November surrounded by her family. She was sixty-two years of age. Tony believes that an internal abscess burst and poisoned her system. Seán adds: 'I have a clear memory of a doctor approaching Dad, asking could they do an autopsy. Dad was very distraught and very angry. His reply to that doctor was something along the lines of "No, if you couldn't fix her when she was alive, there's no point in finding out now. It's too late."'

Seán adds that Brother Kiely, a Christian Brother from Westland Row, had been a regular caller to the house over the thirteen years since they had left school. He says, 'I have a clear memory of him calling to sympathise with Dad and the three of us. I remember him saying it would be impossible to fill that gap at the table that our mother left. Isn't it so true.'

# Chapter 11
## Increasing the Club's Profile

In the late 1960s, *The Irish Times* began to feature 'A Social Sort of Column' written by Eileen O'Brien, a perceptive and empathic journalist. She visited St Vincent's on a busy club night. The article she wrote, 'Youth Behind Bars,' captures the exuberance of the members as well as the concerns of the leaders. She described the club's activities as a way of preventing young people from being 'packed off to Letterfrack, to Daingean or to St Patrick's, Mountjoy', and instead trying 'to divert them from crime to constructive activity'[1].

The absence of suitable club premises was a big issue. *The Irish Times* article indicates some of the restrictions that arise when trying to run a club in an Eastern Health Board dispensary. Unemployment was another worry. 'There is plenty of employment for girls, but when the boys leave school at fourteen there is little for them but to become messengers. Then at eighteen the strong ones get labouring work, but if they are not strong enough for heavy work they may be idle for a very long time,' wrote O'Brien.

---

1. Youth Behind Bars, *The Irish Times*, 11 November 1968.

Other concerns rumble throughout the article. Most club members left school too early. Some emigrated to England and the leaders tried to keep in touch. The recent summer holidays in Knockadoon and Aughrim, while enjoyed greatly, had cost over £700. The article quoted the recently arrived club chaplain, Fr Brian Power, as suggesting alternatives to institutional care for young lawbreakers and the need for a rehabilitation programme. He also said there should be liaison between voluntary workers like those in St Vincent's and official social workers.[2]

'Youth Behind Bars' gives a glimpse of how the St Vincent's leaders, led by Noel, were thinking about the manifold problems facing young people in the area at that time.

### The Kennedy Report

As a Department of Justice employee, Noel was intensely interested in a government-appointed committee set up in 1967. What became known as 'The Kennedy Report' was published in 1970[3]. The initial brief to focus on reformatory and industrial school systems was subsequently extended to cover all children in care.

Noel was aware that another good friend, the Jesuit priest Fr Kenneth McCabe, had been encouraging the Minister for Education, Donogh O'Malley, to take some action on industrial schools. Working in Britain, the priest expressed concern about

---

2. One of the photographs taken by *The Irish Times* photographer on that occasion reappeared in that newspaper's weekend magazine, 'The Times we Lived in', on 23 April 2016. It included club leaders Jim Guider, John Walsh and Terry Kelly, drama teacher Finbar Howard, girls from St Brigid's Club in Irish dancing costumes and boys from St Vincents. Among those photographed are Bernadette Moran, Catherine Russell, Catherine Bernie, Eileen Moran, Katherine Moran, Tina Kennedy, Ann Nolan, Imelda McGuinness, Pauline Ashmore, Maria Archibold, Ann Cannon, Catherine O'Reilly, Catherine Kelly, Geraldine Kerins, Christy Russell.

3. Government of Ireland (1970) *Reformatory and Industrial School Systems* (The Kennedy Report), Dublin: Stationery Office.

the plight of so many young Irish people who had been in reformatory and industrial schools and who ended up in trouble. He suggested 'radical reform of the whole approach to after-care[4]'. Initially, as the Ryan Report[5] records, Fr McCabe was to be included on the committee but subsequently, following a cabinet meeting, his name was deleted.

Chaired by District Justice Eileen Kennedy, the committee consulted widely. The Kennedy Report was refreshingly frank in its conclusions[6]. For example: 'We find the present reformatory system completely inadequate'. It stated unequivocally that the detention centres at Daingean in Co. Offaly and Marlborough House in Dublin should be closed. There was a strong focus on the importance of family, on the prevention of family breakdown and on replacing institutional care with group homes 'that would approximate as closely as possible to the normal family unit.' There were recommendations about developing a proper child care system including aftercare and about the importance of, and right to, education stating that, 'all children in residential care or otherwise should be educated to the ultimate of their capacities.' The age of criminal responsibility, previously starting at age seven, should be raised to twelve years.

The Kennedy Report was enormously relevant for Noel. It related directly to his role in the probation and welfare service and to his voluntary youth work and it offered real hope for change within the

---

4. Commission to Inquire into Child Abuse, Vol IV, p. 305.

5. Ibid. p. 307.

6. When Bertie Ahern in his role of Taoiseach in 1999 made a 'sincere and long overdue apology to the victims of childhood abuse', he referenced the Kennedy Report of nearly thirty years earlier with its assertion that 'All children need love, care and security' and that 'too many of our children were denied this love, care and security'. B. Ahern, 'Bertie Ahern Announces Government Measures Relating to Childhood Abuse', 11 May 1999, archived speeches available on *education.ie*, press room.

system. Noel and the other St Vincent's leaders discussed the report at length. They composed a letter which both *The Irish Times* and the *Irish Independent* published. The letter began by welcoming the apparent public interest in children convicted of offences against the law. It asked how much appetite there was for the abolition or radical reform of the system of institutions and laws for young offenders. It suggested that juvenile delinquency needed to be viewed in a wider context, stating that, 'the elimination, therefore of the chief factors which contribute to lawbreaking among young people should be our first concern'. Factors mentioned included 'poverty, bad housing, parental inadequacy, poor community planning, adult prejudices, unhealthy local rivalries, the influence of companions, television or cinema programmes, dissatisfaction with society – perhaps many more could be listed.'

The St Vincent's letter continued by quoting from the report: 'There is a need for increased support for youth clubs and the provision of trained youth club leaders who would help young people organise their activities and, if possible, involve the parents in these activities.' This was followed by reference to St Vincent's policies including the need for the early identification of 'signs of family distress which so often lead to delinquency'. The letter concluded: 'Perhaps we may incur the customary charge of lack of sympathy with the victims of juvenile crime. Society, it may be cried, must be protected. We agree. Both the potential victims of crime and the present youthful victims of social neglect must be saved before it is too late.'[7]

### New possibilities

That letter indicates a growing confidence among Noel and his St Vincent's club colleagues and reflects many conversations

---

7. The full letter is in *The Irish Times*, 22 January 1971 and is signed by Anne Braine, Noel Clear, Vincent Collins, Gerard Jeffers, Thomas Gilmore, Terry Kelly, and (Fr) Brian Power.

which increasingly sought to understand the causes of poverty and the possibilities of meaningful interventions. While listening carefully, Noel was suspicious of elaborate, utopian solutions; theories needed to be tested against the everyday realities of people's lives. The final demolition of the Keogh Square barracks and news of plans for replacement buildings – to be renamed St Michael's Estate – led the group to imagine new forms of youth work. In addition, events like the annual National Youth Council of Ireland gathering in Red Island, Skerries, Co Dublin energised Noel and sparked further thinking about youth work responses to social problems.

Through his voluntary work, Noel honed a range of skills: organising, supervising, listening, talking, driving and fundraising chief among them. At one stage, he became a DJ for club discos; the family still has boxes of the LPs he used (78s, 45s and 33s), artefacts from a different era. Jim Guider recalls a time when Noel, ably supported by Terry Kelly and other club leaders, ventured into the world of show business. They hired the Rialto Cinema for a fundraising concert; an impressive line-up included entertainer Brendan Grace and the popular all-girl singing trio Maxi, Dick and Twink. While the event didn't lose money, Noel was happy to concentrate on slightly less stressful fundraising events.

### Emerging beliefs

A St Vincent's brochure from the late 1960s illustrates how Noel and colleagues imagined a youth centre. They wrote:

WE BELIEVE ...
- A Youth Centre should be open to all, particularly adolescents with problems;
- Young people should be assisted to develop their personalities and overcome obstacles which inhibit this development;

- A wide variety of activities, cultural, recreational and educational must be provided to suit all temperaments;
- Prevention of delinquency is better than cure or repression.

WE ALSO BELIEVE ...
- Youth cannot be viewed in isolation from the family, for distress in the home means distress for the child. Our youth centre needs a social welfare section to organise employment, counselling and a temporary relief and occasional loan scheme for families in unexpected difficulties;
- People should be helped to support themselves and to understand and obtain assistance to which they are legally entitled;
- We are helping by doing our best to achieve these aims although we have no premises of our own;
- Although we have no capital to extend the work of our welfare section, you can help us and society:
  > By direct involvement in our activities;
  > By continuing your kind support to our annual Christmas and holiday fund;
  > By contribution to our social welfare fund.

Discussion and analysis of issues facing some Inchicore families helped Noel clarify his thinking and deepen his sense of what it meant to be an active Christian. While charity was the central dynamic of his efforts, Noel increasingly worried that responding to people's immediate needs rarely addressed the root causes of problems; he began to realise that charity needs to be complemented by justice. Not everyone agreed and Noel was known to recall the celebrated mantra of Hélder Câmara, a Brazilian archbishop: 'When I give food to the poor, they call me a saint. When I ask why the poor have no food, they call me a communist.' When, more than three decades later, Noel was national president of the SVP, he sometimes revisited lessons learned during those days of discussion and analysis.

## Demolishing the Square

Dublin Corporation began demolishing part of Keogh Square in the early 1960s. This added to the picture of dereliction. In 1967, the corporation decided to knock down the remaining buildings. Initially, according to O'Meara, the plan was to build houses but 'due to pressure from the shopkeepers, who were not willing to have a loss of income for the sake of houses, the corporation opted for high-rise flats instead.'[8] Clearing the last vestiges of the former Richmond Barracks suggested a break with a past characterised by poverty and neglect. A mood of hope and the sense of a fresh start surrounded the building of St Michael's Estate.[9] In recognising new possibilities, Noel also wished to honour the people of the Square. In *The Link* in February 1970, he welcomed the new residents, assuring them that the youth centre was for their benefit. He continued:

> We in St Vincent's Youth Centre will long remember the people of Keogh Square – but not for what certain people often attempted to brand them. Our memory is of the wonderful spirit of unity and generosity that prevailed in the area; of the anxiety of one person to help another; of the tribute to the Catholic faith of the parents who by their weekly subscriptions

8. L. O'Meara, *Who Remembers Keogh Square?* 2016, p. 239.

9. O'Meara notes, 'The history of St Michael's Estate is remarkably similar to that of Keogh Square and it seems that no lessons were learned by any of those concerned' (Ibid, p. 261). St. Michael's Estate was demolished in 2013. A new development, Thornton Heights, was built a year later. In 2016, a museum devoted to 1916 was opened in the former gymnasium of Richmond Barracks/CBS National School.

and active work erected the Shrine to Our Lady against the pessimistic observers who were of the opinion that the Shrine would not last twelve months; of the Trojan work of the Keogh Square Residents Association, the first of such associations in Inchicore, and last but not least the spirit and goodwill that was prevalent among the boys and girls associated with St Vincent's since its foundation in 1957.

Intense engagement with pressing issues forged strong bonds of friendship among conference members and others associated with St Vincent's club. John O'Flaherty, one of the Kimmage students who volunteered in the club recalls how, having departed the seminary but still attending university, he required accommodation. 'I was a country lad, unfamiliar with the city. I remember making a phone call before returning to Dublin after the summer and I was met off the train by a three-person welcoming committee: Noel, John Walsh and Terry Kelly. They organised digs for me out beyond Inchicore. I was very grateful. You never forget friends like that,' he adds.

**The Link**
*The Link,* the club's modestly produced monthly magazine, printed on a Gestetner duplicating machine and sold by club members after Masses in St Michael's Church, continued to profile concerns of Noel and his fellow SVP conference members. *The Link* is also part of Inchicore's own history, reminding readers of the activities of tenants and residents associations, hundreds of local projects as well as glimpses of individual characters. One random example, from the Christmas issue of 1970, includes a 'Know Your Rights' column; an interview with St Patrick's Athletic manager John Colrain; 'Death in Moore Street' by Des McInerney, a prize-winning poem from Inchicore Youth Week; a piece on the value

of pre-marriage courses; a plea for a better deal for young people; a report on the Bulfin Road Senior Citizens group; some cartoons; and an account of young people sleeping rough in the locality. That account states that St Vincent's youth centre was aware of ten young people in the locality who sleep under bushes or in lifts because they had no homes to go to or because of trouble with their parents. 'These children who sleep out present Inchicore with a serious problem. If we do not try to help them now, then tomorrow, they may well be the "down and outs" of our society,' noted the article, inviting readers to respond to the issue.

## Strong memories

Kenny Clarke has strong memories of his childhood in Keogh Square and as a member of St Vincent's:

> Growing up wasn't easy. I had six brothers and six sisters and there wasn't much to go around. Looking back, my Ma must have had a very tough life. The Vincent de Paul conference did a lot for the people in the Square. I remember food parcels at Christmas. And toys, one toy per child. The youth club was a shining light in a pretty dark place. It was one of the few places where we met decent human beings who weren't going to hit us. The leaders were great. The club was the only thing for us young people as we had no money. I got involved in football, drama and table tennis. I regret I never took the opportunity to learn chess. I'm sixty-two now and wonder might I try it?

> We really got to know the leaders well when we went on holidays. Knockadoon was my first one. I'd never been away from home before that. It was great, though I was afraid of the bigger guys. I'd just come out of hospital and didn't want

my stitches opened. I think Noel had a quiet word with the bigger guys and I was okay. There was another holiday in Garron Tower in Antrim and then one in a monastery in Co. Tipperary. I also remember Kerdiffstown, Rathangan and Carne. They were good experiences.

Noel was a really good person, a genuine helpful guy. Later, when I was a senior in the club and after that as a leader, Noel was the person to go to if there was a problem. You were always welcome in number fifty [Tyrconnell Road]. His Da was a very friendly man too. I don't think I can ever remember Noel losing his temper, even raising his voice. He was very calm and there were some tough people in that club. Once, I was playing a match for the club, probably under sixteen, out in Clontarf. One of their guys clattered into my brother Jimmy with a nasty sliding tackle. I looked at Dicey (Reilly) and we both went over and got stuck in. The ref shouted, 'match abandoned' and ran off. A few days later I was up before a CYC[10] disciplinary board. They barred me for life. That was harsh and I lost the head with them. Anyway, Noel made a case in my defence. The ban was reduced to a year. Thanks Noel.

You know he wasn't much of a footballer himself. I can remember occasions when Anne played, usually in goal, and she was much better than Noel. They were a lovely couple Anne and Noel. Noel was generous, always giving, never taking. It's an awful pity he died so young.

---

10. The then Catholic Youth Council (CYC) organised the football leagues in which St Vincent's played.

# Chapter 12
## Supporting, Encouraging, Enabling

Noel viewed his involvement with young people and their families in Inchicore and beyond as one of support and encouragement. He was sympathetic to their situations. Instinctively, he wanted people to help themselves.

However, resilience notwithstanding, Noel was acutely aware of how fragile and vulnerable people can be. He began to see the need for better structures and improved planning. It was also becoming evident that he possessed excellent skills as an organiser, was calm under pressure and, usually, remained on good terms with everyone. How Noel's values resonated with those of St Vincent de Paul and its co-founder Blessed Fréderic Ozanam can be seen through a number of lenses.

### Christmas

Noel's attitude to Christmas was ambivalent. On the one hand, he marvelled at the Christmas story, its serene simplicity and its radical message; on the other, the excesses associated with the festive season made him uncomfortable. The ugliness of poverty is especially stark at that time of year. Throughout his life, the plight of hungry children moved Noel to action. Each Christmas season, volunteers in St Vincent's club assembled and distributed food parcels. This involved approaching local shops and food suppliers for donations. Many were generous. Noel's family home became the nerve centre of the annual operation. In the run up to Christmas, cans of beans, packets of cornflakes, tea and biscuits, jars of jam and marmalade were stacked to the ceiling. Noel demonstrated a great talent for logistics, calm leadership and incisive knowledge about the perishability of certain foodstuffs. In 1969, more than one hundred families in Keogh Square received food hampers.

In later years, the idea of food parcels has been complemented by vouchers for shops and supermarkets, enabling people to choose the food to meet their family's individual circumstances. Within the SVP, the 'appeal' just before Christmas is a high point every year, an opportunity to draw attention to current manifestations of poverty and injustice, to illustrate the work of the society and to invite the public to continue their generous funding. When Noel was SVP national president, his passionate convictions about the cruelty and injustice of hunger and poverty were evident at press conferences, on radio and on TV. In the SVP Bulletin of Spring 2002, Noel recalled an experience the previous Christmas. He wrote of being in a major supermarket close to midnight, observing shoppers manoeuvring trolleys overflowing with all kinds of food. 'It was as if famine was ahead for all,' he remarked. Later, in answer to an emergency call to the SVP head office, Noel called on a woman and her baby in temporary accommodation. The image of the empty fridge at Christmas stuck with him, a reminder of how wealth and poverty often live side by side.

**Caring**

Father Tony Sheridan, a Spiritan missionary working in Brazil since the 1970s, tells a powerful story that illustrates his indebtedness to Noel's care, concern and smart thinking.

> When I was a seminarian in Kimmage, I had been visiting the youth club in Keogh Square and, honestly, I wasn't very comfortable as I didn't know what to do, how to react. When Noel and Fr Brian Power organised classes in the Little Sisters of the Assumption Seven Oaks Convent for the more troublesome kids from the Model School, I was very enthusiastic. I suppose I am a teacher at heart and this was something concrete I could do. There were three children in the class. I prepared the classes well and they made some progress. I was pleased with the results. Every so often Noel or Brian would send in another kid – this disrupted my idea of the class – to help their reading.

Tony puts a heavy emphasis on the phrase 'my idea of the class.' 'This was frustrating for me,' he continues.

> At times, I felt I was wasting my time and the kids' time as some only stayed for one or two classes. I said I thought the class was a waste of time. I'll never forget Brian's response. Tony, he said, the idea of the class time was that the kids would feel, realise, that someone was interested in them. Teaching them reading, while useful, was only an excuse to show them that someone cared about them. This changed my approach radically and I can say it influenced my approach to pastoral work in the future. Results are not that important. People are. Both Brian Power and Noel Clear had a very clear vision of this. It's a matter of balance, I suppose, but valuing the individual is far more important, and, at times, more difficult.

I also learned from watching Noel in operation how to treat, let's say, difficult kids and young people. When I was in Keogh Square I didn't know what to say, what to do, how to behave. Seeing Noel in action, I learned that you didn't have to do anything, just be yourself and be present. When that penny dropped, I felt at ease in the Keogh Squares of life. I am forever grateful for those lessons in how to care.

## Trust

Alice Leahy, a nurse who in 1975 set up Trust – now the Alice Leahy Trust – to provide medical and related services for people who are homeless also remembers Noel as an enabler. 'I first met Noel when visiting people who were homeless and serving time in Mountjoy Prison. Over the years we had many chats around "community" and all that it entails. His humanity and concern was clear to all who crossed his path,' she says. Alice liked the way he didn't stand on ceremony and 'his door was always open.' There was a lot of contact and Alice even remembers babysitting for Anne and Noel 'a lifetime ago'.

Alice tells a story that sheds further light on Noel's way of dealing with people. A young man, Dick, who was using Trust's services had been reared in an institution and had spent twenty years in prison. He had no family and no roots and couldn't read and write. Alice recalls him saying at their first meeting that, 'The saddest day of my life was the day they let me out. Prison was my home'. She continues: 'Noel found him accommodation in a community setting and ensured he had regular visits from St Vincent de Paul volunteers. Noel himself visited him weekly and often took him out to lunch. All of this contact helped Dick to feel at home in his new community.' Alice adds that 'Noel was one of the many special people who crossed my path over the years and it was a real privilege to have known him and his family.'

## Society of St Vincent de Paul

By the 1970s, Noel's activities in St Vincent's club attracted attention beyond Inchicore. His flair for organisation led to invitations to join the umbrella bodies for youth work in the city. He was a strong, constructive, practical presence at committee meetings of the Catholic Youth Council, Comhairle le leas Óige[1] and the youth clubs section of the Society of St Vincent de Paul. Noel felt especially at home in the SVP, identifying with its strong tradition of assisting the poor in the city. As Archbishop Diarmuid Martin told SVP volunteers in 2008:

> The Saint Vincent de Paul Society has been a beacon of what living out Christian love means in Ireland and in a special way in Dublin for generations, in good times and in bad and especially in the various periods of particularly bad times, when extreme poverty was a widespread characteristic of our city and diocese. The city and the diocese owe a great debt to your quiet generosity and commitment.[2]

For anyone curious about the archbishop's reference to generations of Dubliners, a short Pathé News film from 1942 is worth viewing.[3] In the pre-television era, Pathé News reports were screened in cinemas, accompanying the main feature film. The commentary accompanying 'City Fathers, Good Work Dublin Issue', captures some of the essence of the SVP:

---

1. Comhairle le leas Óige was the name of a sub-committee of the City of Dublin Vocational Education Committee founded in 1943, renamed City of Dublin Youth Service Board (CDYSB) in the mid-1990s.

2. *Tougher Times – Tender Hearts*, homily by Archbishop Diarmuid Martin, Archbishop of Dublin and Primate of Ireland, St Vincent de Paul Dublin Regional Conference, Croke Park, 8 November 2008.

3. Available at *https://youtu.be/wRG-CbUgE1w*

In some of these slum areas, the poor people have good reason to bless the name of the Society of St Vincent de Paul. We are not able to show you much of the society's work because its members shrink from any form of publicity, but we can give you a brief outline. The city fathers, as they are affectionately called, help people who cannot help themselves. Sometimes they adopt families and look after all their needs. That voucher – we can only show the hand that writes it – makes all the difference. There's a poor girl, for instance, who was without shoes until one of the city fathers adopted her and provided her with a voucher that enabled her to get them. A boy is in need of clothes so another voucher is his passport to a complete rig-out. All these things are gifts, gifts from more fortunate people who give heed to the lot of the poor and especially poor children. Properly shod with a pair of stout boots and the owner of a good suit, a youngster quickly regains his self-respect. He can now face the battle of life with confidence and, if he's old enough, he will get a job. You can easily imagine that the work of the city fathers of the Society of St Vincent de Paul is very heavy. With the approach of winter the needs of the poor have increased considerably. Why not help the Society to meet those needs? You would be doing a great and urgent service.

## Founder

The Society of St Vincent de Paul was founded by Fréderic Ozanam in 1833. Ozanam was a twenty-year-old student at the Sorbonne in Paris when he and some friends came together to form a group of volunteers to assist poor people. The initial group worked under the guidance of Sr Rosalie Rendu, a Daughter of Charity.

Naming the group after Vincent de Paul was an acknowledgement of that saint's inspiring vision. Vincent de

Paul, a priest, had ministered in Paris in the early seventeenth century. He had a special concern for the poor and marginalised. There was extensive wealth in Paris and those who went hungry, who begged in the street or were homeless, were often despised. The sick – there was no state health service then – children and refugees were among the most vulnerable. Many of those whom Vincent met had lost hope. He saw each person created in the image of God. However, he was frustrated and angry that their dignity as human beings was being eroded. He wished to be practical in his responses, doing his best to ease people's suffering.

Vincent has been described as innovative and pragmatic, honest and approachable, realistic and visionary, opportunistic and a risk-taker. He was values driven and hardworking, intelligent yet blessed with common sense. It is no coincidence that people who remember Noel frequently use similar words. Biographers describe Vincent de Paul's communication style as simple, straightforward and powerfully persuasive. Prayerful and contemplative, he was equally comfortable in the presence of a queen or beggar. This profoundly Christian man was also good at enlisting the support of other men and women to the cause of the poor.

One such colleague was Louise de Marillac, a widow and mother, who, with Vincent, went on to found the Daughters of Charity. Members of that congregation are today working in over ninety different countries. Louise was declared a saint in 1934 and, in 1960, Pope John XXIII declared her the patron saint of social workers. Vincent, along with five other priests, founded the Congregation of the Mission, known today in Ireland as The Vincentians or Vincentian Fathers.[4] Vincent also initiated other religious groups, including the Ladies of Charity and the

---

4. Vincentians in Ireland founded All Hallows College, a Dublin seminary, St Patrick's College Drumcondra for the education of primary teachers, St Paul's College Raheny and Castleknock College, two secondary schools in Dublin. Vincentians also minister in St Peter's Parish, Phibsboro Dublin.

Confraternities of Charity. All these groups shared a common mission to serve people in need and transform the world for the better. Vincent de Paul died in 1660.[5] Sadly, poverty and injustice, to which he responded so well, is just as problematic in the twenty-first century.

## Ireland

When Ozanam and friends founded the Society of St Vincent de Paul, Paris was recovering from a severe outbreak of cholera and poverty was rampant. When the group met in the Church of Saint-Sulpice in Paris, the goal was simple enough: set up a 'Conference of Charity' and through it offer practical charitable help to the poor as an expression of their Catholic faith. Soon, they were visiting poor families across Paris as well as meeting and praying together. Within a decade there were over ten thousand SVP volunteers throughout France.

Eleven years after its Paris foundation, the first Irish SVP Conference formed in Dublin. According to a recent book[6] marking one-hundred-and-seventy years of the SVP in Ireland, a striking feature of the organisation has been how it has adapted to meet changing social and economic conditions brought about by famine, two world wars, civil war, internal strife, boom times and years of austerity. The core activity of home visits has been complemented by hostels, resources centres, shops, visitation of the sick and imprisoned.

The society's campaigning for social justice was stepped up in 1980 with the publication of 'Old and Alone in Ireland'[7], a survey that found that 30 per cent of older people had no flush toilets,

---

5. Vincent de Paul was declared a saint in 1737.

6. *The Society of St Vincent de Paul in Ireland: 170 Years of Fighting Poverty*, edited by Bill Lawlor and Joe Dalton, Dublin: New Island Books, 2014.

7. B. Power, *Old and Alone in Ireland: A Report on a Survey of Old People Living Alone*, Dublin: Society of St Vincent de Paul, 1980.

hot water or hand basins in their homes and more than one third never met anyone on a daily basis. This data-gathering exercise gave the SVP a solid platform from which to advocate for policy changes by government, to go beyond charity and handouts. The shift reflected evolving thinking in the wider Church. As the Synod of Bishops put it in 1971:

> Christian love of neighbour and justice cannot be separated. For love implies an absolute demand for justice, namely a recognition of the dignity and right of one's neighbour. Justice attains its inner fullness only in love.[8]

## Youth work enabler

One illustration of Noel's capacity for enabling others was his support for Comhairle le Leas Óige youth workers in the early 1970s. The youth organisation had begun to employ community youth officers. As Maurice Ahern noted in 1975:

> Contact with some of the youth could be made through youth clubs but the majority of youngsters were to be found on the streets and roads so contact was made with them there. By meeting and talking to them on the streets the youth officer got to know them personally, got to know their background, their attitudes, their lifestyle and their problems. Over a period of time relationships developed, culminating in help on various problems being requested by the young people. Having a centrally located office in the area, facilitated good communication not only with young people, but also with

---

8. Synod of Bishops (1971) *Justice in the World.* Paragraph 34. This document also states clearly (para. 6) 'Action on behalf of justice and participation in the transformation of the world fully appear to us as a constitutive dimension of the preaching of the Gospel, or, in other words, of the Church's mission for the redemption of the human race and its liberation from every oppressive situation'.

many agencies and organisations whose help and co-operation were vital to the job.[9]

Derry O'Connor began working as a full-time youth worker in the Crumlin area of Dublin in 1972. 'I was not long out of college. We had very few resources. A lot of the work depended on using our wits, connecting with youngsters on the streets. Two supports in particular made my job a lot easier. One was the recent availability of Free Legal Advice Centre (FLAC)[10] and the other was Noel Clear,' he says. Derry explains that many of the young people he worked with were regularly in trouble with the law and so were frequently incarcerated in St Patrick's Institution or Mountjoy Prison:

> With his own background in voluntary youth work, Noel had a clear vision of what youth workers like Maurice Ahern, Peter Mooney, Noel Coughlan and myself were trying to do. Hence, he facilitated us to visit these young people in prison. He smoothed the way, opened doors that had previously been closed. This helped us enormously. We were able to maintain links with our client group when they were locked up; he facilitated continuity. That was vital. We were able to help them prepare for life afterwards. I think of Noel as an enabler. Then, and afterwards, he made things happen, that was the kind of guy he was. This he did in a quiet way. He never let ego get in the way. He was working in an oppressive system but he was an enlightened person. He never wrote people

9. M. Ahern, *Youth Work in Dublin: Towards an Integrated Approach.* Comhairle le Leas Óige, 1975.

10. Free Legal Advice Centres was started by a group of law students looking to use their legal knowledge and provide advice and information to those who could not afford the fees involved. David Byrne, Denis McCullough, Vivian Lavan and Ian Candy set up the organisation in April 1969. Further information is available at *www.flac.ie*

off so was always willing to give interventions a chance. He trusted us. He was never judgemental, never inquisitorial. I owe him a lot. He was, I suppose, avuncular in his manner, caring and supportive.

# Chapter 13
## A Life-Changing Experience

'Maybe it's time to find yourself a wife and settle down.' Jack Clear, Noel's father, was a practical, down-to-earth man. He sometimes wondered aloud whether Noel was spending too much of his spare time with the youth club. Jack was especially happy when Noel accompanied him to the pub, usually Dillon's (also known as The Black Lion) on Emmet Road. There he would often remind Noel that he was more than thirty years of age, and hence no longer a 'spring chicken'.

Traditionally SVP had been an all-male organisation, reflecting the nineteenth century context of its origins. In the Dublin archdiocese, women members were welcomed from 1962 onwards. Many benefits resulted and one was especially personal for Noel. Anne Braine, bright and vivacious, working then in the Office of the Minister for Transport and Power, was one of the first women to join St Vincent's conference. Anne had grown up in Drimnagh, adjacent to Inchicore. She knew Inchicore and its people well. She babysat regularly for Vincent and Marie Collins who lived on Kickham Road. Vincent was a member of the conference and suggested that Anne would be a good addition. 'I went along at Vincent's suggestion and I was very struck by the vibrancy, the energy among the conference members. It also opened my eyes to another side of life,' says Anne.

Jim Guider, another volunteer leader and close friend of Noel, has a vivid recollection of Noel's reaction to Anne.

For years he had been very single-minded in his dedication to the youth club. We would go to dances and pubs together but Noel was often more focused on the music than the girls. He was shy. There weren't many girlfriends that I recall. Shortly after Anne joined the conference, Noel confided in me that he was thinking of asking her out on a date. I could see he was very attracted to her but unsure about making a move. One day he was going on a bit about it as we drove along Dorset Street so I stopped the car outside a telephone kiosk. I actually dialled the number and handed him the phone. 'Go on, ask her,' I said.

Discreetly, Noel and Anne began going out together. The Purty Kichen in Dún Laoghaire was a favourite meeting place. The April 1972 issue of *The Link* carries a brief announcement of their engagement. The wedding took place on 1 September in the Oblate Church on Tyrconnell Road. Their good friend Fr Brian Power, recently transferred from Inchicore to Bray, and Fr Willie Morrisey, Anne's uncle, officiated. The reception was held in the Killiney Heights Hotel, a venue now long demolished and replaced by apartments.

'We went on our honeymoon to Devon and Cornwell in England,' remembers Anne. 'As we were in the vicinity, Noel, being Noel, couldn't resist the idea of visiting the famous prison at Dartmoor. So off we trekked. Noel was fascinated, obviously comparing and contrasting it to Mountjoy and St Patrick's in Dublin. I'd say we are in the small minority of people who visited a prison on their honeymoon,' she laughs.

Subsequently, Noel and Anne lived in Tyrconnell Road along with Jack. While getting married was life-changing and life-enhancing, the experience didn't deflect Noel from his beloved St Vincent's Club, especially as new challenges were appearing on the horizon. Back in 1971, the Eastern Health Board had terminated their stay in the dispensary that had been the club's base for many years. Noel's campaign for a purpose-built youth centre gathered momentum. A building fund was established. Lots of local meetings took place. The Planning Department of Dublin Corporation agreed, in principle, on a site for the centre. Fundraising became a priority.

**Waste paper**

In the early 1970s, collecting waste paper was one effective fundraising activity. Father Jimmy Nolan, an Oblate priest based in St Michael's, led the waste paper collection campaign. 'Jimmy's garage and Noel's garage were used to store the paper,' recalls Jim Guider who, along with Terry Kelly, John Geoghegan and John O'Brien from Bulfin, organised club members into collecting teams. This activity raised valuable funds for the new centre. Jim recalls that on at least one occasion Noel and himself discovered that some enterprising youngsters were collecting on their own behalf and selling directly to the waste paper company. They laughed but put a quick halt to the practice! The waste paper collection ran until 1978. The team also put energy into a Green Shield Stamps[1] campaign. A weekly disco for teenagers generated further contributions. So too did the Sunday night bingo session. Club members put on a spectacular performance of *Joseph and the Amazing Technicolor Dreamcoat*. Critically, Noel was instrumental in securing a grant of £25,000 from the SVP towards the centre.

---

1. This was a scheme that rewarded shoppers with stamps which could then be used to acquire gifts from a catalogue. Gifts could also be obtained by a combination of stamps and cash. In the 1990s the stamps were discontinued and the operation was rebranded as Argos.

Meanwhile, club activities, including the demanding but much loved summer holidays – to Carne, Kerdiffstown, Brosna – continued with Noel centrally involved. The first summer project in Inchicore started in 1975 with Catherine Kelly as co-ordinator. An Inchicore Community Council also kicked off in the mid-1970s. Noel also succeeded in involving Finbar Howard, a gifted teacher of drama, once again with St Vincent's. For example, 'I am a Rocker' written by Mick Nolan and John Wall and set to music by Niall Dempsey was a big hit with local fans.

## New building

The new youth centre building was eventually completed in 1976. In preparation for the next stage, the conference organised a weekend seminar for youth leaders. This was led by the late Peter Mooney, training officer of Comhairle le Leas Óige. In 1977, Lord Mayor Michael Collins officially opened the new premises and Bishop Dermot O'Mahony blessed it. There were some teething problems with security but soon the centre was functioning more or less along the lines imagined by Noel and his colleagues. By any yardstick, this was a major achievement. When Noel and Jerry O'Sullivan began the club in a small room in Keogh Square in 1958, in their wildest imaginings they could not have foreseen such a solid, substantial, modern, well-resourced facility for young people. To this day, that building remains a very tangible part of Noel's extensive legacy.

## Chapter 14
# Full and Busy Days

'It's a boy!' Rory's birth in July 1973 brought great joy to Anne and Noel as well as to their extended families.

On top of his work in the probation and welfare service, Noel continued to drive efforts for the youth centre, maintained his engagement with various organisations beyond Inchicore as well as enjoying family life with Anne, Rory and Rory's grandfather, Jack. Each day was busy and full but Noel began to consider an even more demanding regime.

As the probation and welfare service began to expand, most new recruits were graduates with degrees in the social sciences. Noel had attended various short courses in the Dublin Institute of Adult Education and his appetite was whetted. Now that he was in a supervisory role, he wondered about gaining further qualifications. Letters from Jerry O'Sullivan in South America, now enrolled as a doctoral student in Stanford University, was a further spur. Noel wrote to various universities in Ireland and Britain and conducted an extended correspondence with Professor Conor Ward in the Department of Social Science in UCD.

The letters reveal the frightening extent to which universities at that time were inflexibly rule-bound. Noel could not be admitted to the Diploma in Social Science or the Diploma in Applied Social Science. Noel's spirited reply questioned how those with no experience could be accepted, while someone like him with many years professional and voluntary social work could be excluded. Conor Ward's frustration with the regulations is obvious in the correspondence, noting that he and his colleagues had been advocating courses for 'persons like yourself'. Eventually and reluctantly, Noel gave up on that idea, though he continued to read widely on the subject.

Working alongside him, Tom Gilmore remembers Noel having confidence in his own ability. 'It didn't particularly bother him that someone had a degree in psychology or sociology, though he respected that. Indeed, he was often disappointed with the limited insights of such people,' remarks Tom. He makes the point that probation work is so much about having one's heart in the right place. 'Clients are very quick to see through people. They detect caring and regard for people, or its absence. Noel had a great facility to communicate warmth and to build up people's self-confidence. It was like a rule of his life,' adds Tom.

Tom McSweeney, who edited the SVP Bulletin for over twenty years, also held Noel in high esteem. When Tom joined the society in the 1970s, he was following in the steps of his grandfather who had been a member in the 1920s. Tom's wife Kathleen was also an SVP member. In their home in Monkstown, Cork, there is a framed photograph of Noel as national president presenting Kathleen with a medal for twenty-five years' service. Skilfully, the framer has incorporated the actual medal into the picture. Tom, like other volunteers, has many anecdotes of his time in SVP conferences in Dublin and Cork. He admired Noel very much, particularly his efforts to bring social justice to the centre of the society's work. 'I recall Noel's insistence that "you must always listen to people,"' says Tom. 'He was always determined to see the individual person. He didn't have much time for terms like "clients," "service-users" or "the poor". Noel was a guy who really listened'. Tom, whose distinctive and distinguished voice many remember from his work as RTÉ's southern editor and as presenter of the *Seascapes* radio programme, also recalls Noel's wry sense of humour. These two qualities, listening and humour, were central features of Noel's personality.

## The spectre of drug abuse

In 1976 Noel's good friend Fr Brian Power returned to Ireland having completed a master's degree in social work research in Boston College. Appointed to Dún Laoghaire parish, Brian quickly became involved in responding to the emerging drug abuse problems there. He recalled that, 'We wrote letters to various government departments. I was surprised that there was no response from health or education but we did hear from the Department of Justice. That response came through the probation and welfare service. I remember Noel's colleague Martin Tansey saying, "These young people are our responsibility". Of course, Noel was very supportive. He was like that, never censorious, always seeing the human side.' Unfortunately, despite early warnings from concerned people on the ground, drug abuse soon became a cancer in the country, destroying many lives, devastating communities and altering that lawbreaking landscape. The epidemic also brought new challenges for the probation service, for youth work and for the SVP.

## Family

Rory's brother Alan was born in January 1976 to the delight of Noel and Anne and the wider family. Two young children with self-selected sleeping times didn't mix well with Noel's external commitments. It was not unknown for Noel to strap one of the wide-awake boys into the car and drive around the city in the hope of lulling him to sleep.

Two children became three in 1981 with Conor's arrival. The three boys' memories of their childhood are peppered with warm accounts of their parents. Noel's focused attention to his work is recalled fondly. 'When you'd go out with him, he always seemed to bump into people he knew. Everyone seemed to be either in trouble with the law or associated with the Vincent de Paul,' says Rory. The boys even invented their own game which they called 'going to meetings', reflecting Noel's extensive evening commitments. The Dublin Mountains, especially the Hell Fire Club on Montpelier Hill, south of Tallaght, was a popular venue for family excursions.

Another phenomenon the boys remember was the unexpected caller. 'Sometimes people who had been in prison and might have been a bit lost called to the house,' remembers Rory. He recounts an occasion, after Christmas, when 'a guy recently released from prison' accompanied Noel and the boys to Funderland in the RDS, having first enjoyed a meal with the family.

Stories of Noel's various cars evoke some hilarious memories. Volkswagen Beetles – two beige models and one bright yellow – were an early preference. 'He then changed to a silver Vauxhall Chevette and it was nothing but trouble,' says Anne. 'These were all second-hand cars and he wasn't at all mechanically minded.' On one summer trip to Skerries with the boys, Anne, Noel and Anne's father all on board, the Chevette struggled to get up a minor hill. 'We all had to get out and push,' she smiles. The next car, a gold Volkswagen Passat Estate, entered family folklore following a memorable outing. Rory takes up the story:

It was the summer of 1984 or 1985 and Dad and myself were driving to see Dublin playing in Croke Park. Noel used get a ticket from his friend Paddy Culloty with whom he worked. The car must have been in some state of disrepair because somewhere past North King Street, a door fell off. I don't know what caused that but it must have been fairly shaky. I don't know if it was my anxiety to get to Croke Park or the fact that he wasn't too pushed about the car, but we didn't abandon the mission to go to the match. There was a garage in Dorset Street, no longer there, and the guy there said it was okay to leave the car in the forecourt. After the match, the car was still there. Nobody had bothered to touch it.

Ironically, Noel had been offered a reasonable price for that car but eventually had to pay to have the clapped-out wreck towed away. Noel's sons laugh further as they recall other dodgy cars – a blue Toyota, a gold Toyota and a green Carina hatchback – debating about which had the single windscreen wiper.

Noel was reconciled to having his car 'borrowed' on occasions. More than once, the vehicle was 'found' in Keogh Square. He even had a story about walking along Tyrconnell Road one day when a young lad rolled down the window and shouted out, 'just leaving your car back, Noel'. Preoccupied with many matters, Noel was prone to forgetfulness. Once, on his way home, he pulled up outside a local newsagent, made his purchases and walked the short distance home. The next morning, seeing no car outside the house, Noel reported it to the Gardaí as missing. Embarrassingly, it was later discovered, still outside the newsagents.

An even more bizarre incident occurred when Conor was about eight years old. 'We pulled into a petrol station on the Crumlin Road. He went in to pay for the petrol and I got out to get something in the shop. He came back to the car and didn't notice that I wasn't there and drove off. I remember him saying afterwards that he was just chatting away to me, thinking I was in the back seat.

Eventually, when there was no response, it dawned on him that I wasn't there. He rushed back. In reality, it was probably only a few minutes but long enough for me to get a big fright,' says Conor.

Alan remembers that when they were young, packing large numbers of kids into the car was very common. Rory recalls bowling events for youth clubs in which himself and Alan, along with friends Declan and David Owens, Gareth and Barry Leonard and Darren Whelan, all piled into one car. 'Nowadays that would contravene health and safety regulations,' remarks Rory. 'One year, as he was an organiser of the event, we had the trophies in the car on the way out. Then we won the competition so we also had them in the car on the way back,' he laughs. 'Anytime I meet Darren Whelan, he still mentions that.'

Alan recalls a time when Noel brought Rory, himself and some friends to an adventure centre in County Wicklow. 'We were in a boat on this little lake. I'd say the water wasn't very deep. There were about five or six of us in the boat and we started rocking it and Dad fell overboard in his shirt and trousers. He hadn't a change of clothes either. We had a good laugh at that,' he says.

### An eye-opening trip to Paris

In October 1976, as part of a French-Irish Youth Exchange Agreement, Geoffrey Corry of the National Youth Council led seven representatives of Irish Youth organisations on a study visit to Paris.[1] The purpose was to learn about French policies and practices in youth, sport, health and social action. Much of the time was spent on the ground in three 'new' towns on the periphery of Paris.

---

1. The seven were: Geoffrey Corry, Derry O'Connor, Liam Clare (Dublin Corporation), Mary Doyle (Catholic Youth Council), Peter Burling (Catholic Youth Council) Fr Seamus Heaney (GAA Ard Comhairle na nÓg and advisory committee to the Co Meath VEC adult education project) and Noel Clear. In the final report Noel is described as Vice-President Council of Youth Clubs of Society of St Vincent de Paul. President of Inchicore Youth Centre. Full-time social worker in Prison Service.

'I sat beside Noel on the flight over,' recalls Derry O'Connor then of Comhairle le Leas Óige. 'I remember him sitting down, tightening his seat belt and rubbing his hands saying he could relax now as the main business of the trip had been completed: he had acquired a present for Anne in the duty free. Perfume, I think.'

It was a busy schedule. There were numerous meetings and receptions, as well as the visits to youth facilities. Despite being on his first visit to Paris, Noel took on the role of unofficial guide as the Irish group navigated their way around the Metro. How did he do? 'Well, we didn't get lost,' says Derry. Highlights of the visit were trips to the 'new' towns of Evry, south of Paris; Sarcelles, north of the city; as well as to Athis-Mons near Orly Airport. In each case the Irish delegation saw at first hand the social circumstances of these communities and how youth work was responding.

As often happens on such study trips, massive amounts of new information were taken on board. The Irish contingent discussed how various ideas and projects might translate into Irish situations. French government support for youth work, opportunities for formal youth work qualifications and the various manifestations of youth work in Paris all impressed the visitors. There were 'mille clubs' – one thousand quick-build pre-fabricated buildings where young people could get together. There were also social centres, playgrounds, youth centres, hostels for young workers. Some activities were targeted at groups such as youth 'at risk', children not in formal education, potential 'delinquents', immigrant children and so on.

Reports from this visit illustrate clearly a French view of youth work as an educational activity, complementing and at times substituting for formal schooling. Integrating young people into the community rather than seeing them as a group apart was also a priority. Noel showed a special interest in how voluntary youth workers worked side-by-side with professional colleagues. Professional youth workers employed as 'street educators' working in an informal manner also caught the visitors' imaginations. So too did the prevention-focused, alcohol-free youth café in Athis-Mons which employed five people full-time. This approach mirrored the innovation that was happening in Dublin at the time, facilitated in no small way by Noel. The Irish observers noted how sporting facilities need to be complemented by opportunities for other forms of self-expression including arts, crafts, music and drama. The role of the Churches in developing youth work, in partnership with the state, was also striking.

'It was very stimulating for all of us. We were excited at the possibility that some of these ideas might be adapted for use in Ireland,' remembers Derry. 'Trips like this are very valuable in helping you clarify what you think of the situation at home. I think we all grew a lot during that week in our understanding of what youth work can offer a society,' he adds.

## Language

Alongside the demands of work, home and voluntary work, Noel remained an active Irish language enthusiast, building on his positive school experiences. He loved opportunities to converse *as Gaeilge* though he was never imposing. 'We never liked the label "Gaeilgeoir"' remarks Seán. 'But I can put on record that Noel was a true *Gaeilgeoir*. We were not fanatics but whenever we had the opportunity we spoke Irish to one another. If we were in the company of people who had little Irish we would speak English,' he says. Noel maintained good links with Seosamh O Broin and Craobh Inse Chór, being an active committee member for many years. Noel's wife Anne also became involved in the Conradh and in the mid-1980s became a teacher in the *naíonra* there, where she still works. Noel and Anne's cultural interest often brought them to Comhaltas Ceoltóirí Éireann in Monkstown on a Friday evening. On occasion, Noel contributed to *Cursaí an Lae* on Radio na Gaeltachta. When he became a regional and later national leader of the SVP, journalists seeking interviews with fluent Irish speakers appreciated his clarity and directness.

# Chapter 15
## Beyond Inchicore

As the reputation of St Vincent's Youth Centre grew, Noel was invited to share his ideas at conferences, discussions and on committees. He accepted requests to join both the Catholic Youth Council (CYC) and the SVP Council of Youth Clubs. Noel's commitment to social justice was palpable. His track record in voluntary work and in the probation service increased his credibility. At meetings, his calm manner and conciliatory tone generated trust and enabled decisions to be taken. 'Noel was a fine man with a great social conscience,' says the then Director of the CYC, Fr John Fitzpatrick. 'He had an independence of mind and a genuine honesty which allowed me to trust him and to have confidence in his judgement and in his opinions,' he adds.

In a 1979 issue of *The Link*, Noel returns to a favourite theme. He begins by recalling current headlines relating to youth and vandalism, cataloguing some grim statistics. Typically, Noel acknowledges the problem, dismisses 'quick fix' solutions and then poses the question, 'what are you going to do about it?' He concludes:

What can society do about the problem? Some say lock up the culprits. What, however, about constructive alternatives? Given a new challenge, perhaps some of our young people might respond and make a useful contribution to our society. Perhaps too often the adult population tend to turn their backs on the reality of the problems facing them.

A few months later, again in *The Link*, Noel reminds readers of the significance of Easter and the anniversary of the 1916 Rising and concludes with an insight on patriotism:

> Today we need a different form of patriotism. Everyone is a potential patriot. To commit ourselves in full to whatever undertaking we have in hand is the task of all. Whether in your work, your family circle or your local community, your interest and dedication to what you are doing should prove a major contribution to the development of your country.

The anniversary of Pádraig Pearse's birth led Noel to remember Pearse the educationalist, recalling his view that 'each school must have freedom to shape its own programme' and that 'inspiration must come from the teacher'. Noel also recalled that Pearse was a committed Catholic with 'a tremendous belief in God', an Irishman who loved Ireland, and an Irish language enthusiast, a *Gaeilgeoir*. He ended with the observation that, 'Pearse has much to contribute to the Irish nation of today'.

## Council of Youth Clubs

His Inchicore experiences had convinced Noel of the value of vibrant youth clubs. The SVP Council of Youth Clubs was a forum where those running clubs under an SVP banner came together to share experiences, plan joint activities and learn from each other. In the late 1960s, Philip Furlong was president of the particular Council for Boys' Clubs and remembers Noel's contributions well. 'I had actually first heard Noel speak as far back as 1961, at a talk about youth work in the Institute of Adult Education in Mountjoy Square. He was in the Legion of Mary at that time and I was impressed with his ideas,' he recalls. Philip was a young civil servant then, not long out of school, and a volunteer in St Benedict's Boys Club in the Liberties. 'I had been in the "yellow berets" for the Patrician Year[1] and arising from that there was a lot of encouragement for us to get involved in some form of social work. Along with other CBS Synge Street past students, I became very involved in organising activities, football teams, annual holidays in St Benedict's. It was both demanding and satisfying,' he recalls. 'Within the Council of Youth Clubs, Noel was challenging. He had a vision. Youth work for him was more than being busy organising activities. He helped us see youth clubs in a broader context, supporting families, a form of community development. Some people didn't like what he was saying, preferring to focus on club activities. Noel was also instrumental in getting us to broaden our thinking by linking with other youth organisations such as the National Youth Council, the Catholic Youth Council and Comhairle Le Leas Óige. He was an important player in developing SVP youth work,' says Philip.

In time, leaders in clubs as diverse as those in Rialto, Ballymun and Bonnybrook came to appreciate Noel's vision and organisational abilities. He was elected to lead the Council of Youth Clubs in the late 1970s and this increased his profile within the SVP organisation.

In 1988, the Council of Youth Clubs marked their first quarter of a century with an event in Dublin. Noel invited the Jesuit

---

1. The Patrician Congress, marking the 1500th anniversary of the death of St Patrick, took place in Dublin in June 1961. Many reports on the events note the presence of the Congress Volunteer Corps of fifth and sixth year schoolboys in distinct uniforms of dark trousers, white shirts and striking yellow berets. Following the Congress, the volunteers subsequently became the Archbishop's Volunteer Corps, involved in various projects across Dublin and also included girl members.

priest and social justice activist, Peter McVerry, to address the gathering along with Seán Curran, the first president of the Youth Clubs Council and Bill Cleary the head of SVP in Dublin. Peter McVerry challenged the SVP volunteer youth leaders to be creative, particularly when some young people were being excluded from the very services that were set up for them. This was a theme close to Noel's heart. He reminded those present of the SVP core remit: 'serving the deprived and disadvantaged'.

## Regional Council

Don Mahony chaired the Dublin Regional Council of the SVP from 1976 until 1981. 'Most of us came from a background of conferences that were involved in visitations, weekly visits to people in their homes where we listened to people's stories and tried to respond to their material needs. Coming from the world of youth clubs, Noel brought a different perspective. I thought many of those youth clubs were doing great work. Noel was very generous in the time and effort he gave to the work,' adds Don.

Between 1981 and 1987, when Don served as SVP national president, they continued to work together following Noel's election as president of the Dublin Regional Council. 'A nicer guy you couldn't meet,' is Don's recollection of Noel. Don vividly recalls how the 1980s were bleak and had a strong impact on those with few resources. Youth unemployment rose, drug addiction grew and social problems in some communities increased. The services offered by SVP volunteers became even more relevant.

One initiative that engaged Noel strongly was a job finders co-op set up by the SVP Council for Youth Clubs in 1989. This was in response to high unemployment rates and aimed to build on the SVP tradition of practical help by providing more structured assistance. Limited verbal skills and difficulties in self-expression were recognised as needs of young jobseekers. A register was drawn up and secretarial support for CVs provided. A phone service was available – this was an era before mobile phones when waiting lists for the installation of landlines could stretch to months – and the co-op offered advice and guidance. There were also links with Comhairle le Leas Óige which provided courses on interview skills.

Noel's consistent belief was that if a young person could get started in a job, a lot of other problems melted away. In the first year, approaches to one thousand seven hundred employers led to eighty interviews and twenty-eight actual jobs, a reminder of how much effort was required to land a single job. Funding for the project, £25,000, was from the SVP Central Council and 'People in Need'.[2] Those implementing the project stated, 'we would especially like to thank Noel Clear for the vision and tenacity to get the co-op up and running.'

## Advice sought

A further indicator of Noel's growing reputation was a letter, received out of the blue in 1984, from Apostolic Nuncio, Gaetano Alibrandi. Dermot Ryan, Archbishop of Dublin since 1972 and successor to Archbishop McQuaid, had been appointed to head up the Congregation for the Evangelisation of Peoples in Rome.[3] The letter invited Noel to suggest three names who would be 'worthy and suitable' for the position of archbishop, 'taking into consideration the particular needs of the archdiocese'. This was a confidential process though there was widespread speculation in the media.

The cover of *Magill* magazine in June 1984 reads 'The Battle for the Diocese of Dublin' with photographs of Archbishop

---

2. 'People in Need' was an RTÉ fundraiser for good causes. It ran every second year from 1989 to 2007 and those ten telethons raised about €35 million. The money was distributed through the People in Need Trust.

3. Dermot Ryan died in Rome a few months later in February 1985. He was sixty years of age.

Ryan flanked by Bishops Eamonn Casey and Dermot O'Mahony, possible successors. In an insightful article entitled 'The Legacy of Dermot Ryan', journalist Olivia O'Leary lists selected names being discussed among some of the nine hundred and seventy-five Dublin diocesan priests and 'interested laity' who had been consulted by the nuncio. In addition to Bishops Casey and O'Mahony, she mentions Bishops Joe Cassidy, Donal Murray, James Kavanagh, Kevin McNamara, Monsignor Desmond Williams, Fr Peter Lemass and Fr John Magee. In *The Irish Times*[4] in July, John Cooney also speculated that Bishop Brendan Comiskey was in the running.

Following the various consultations with clergy and laity, the Bishop of Kerry, Kevin McNamara, became the new archbishop of Dublin. He died three years later and was succeeded by Desmond Connell.[5] It is not clear whether Noel was consulted regarding that appointment.

### Public voice

Noel's growing focus on structural causes of poverty led him to call for public policies to ensure that poor people are not further marginalised. While arguing from the moral perspective of solidarity with disadvantaged people, he also recognised the power of utilitarian viewpoints: less poverty is likely to lead to less crime; greater participation in school leads to a better educated workforce; increased employability contributes to greater productivity and so on. Ultimately, action to combat poverty can lead to greater social stability, to a more even distribution of society's riches and to the common good.

There are echoes of Noel's thinking in Archbishop Martin's 2008 homily to SVP volunteers when he said:

---

4. 7 July 1984.

5. Coincidentally, like his predecessor, Archbishop McNamara was also sixty years of age when he died.

A poverty strategy at times of cut-backs must not just focus, then, on the effects on the poor today, but above all must have as a priority ensuring that the poor maintain those possibilities they have of enhancing their human potential – I am thinking of education and health care – so that when times get better they can emerge rapidly as active and productive subjects of their own and our own future. Reducing the opportunity of the poor in times of crisis may well be condemning them to exclusion also in times when thing improve.

Archbishop Martin concluded his remarks saying:

We thank God that in good times and in bad the tender hearts of the Saint Vincent de Paul Society are always there, discreetly and in an undemonstrative way, bringing something extra, not just in financial terms, but in the unique warmth that comes from the community who believe that God is love.[6]

### Social structures

Over the years, Noel's thinking regarding poverty shifted as he attempted to localise the application of the Gospels. The 1971 Synod of Bishops put it like this:

It is up to Christian communities to analyse with objectivity the situation which is proper to their own country, to shed on it the light of the Gospel's unalterable words and to draw principles of reflection, norms of judgement and directives for action.[7]

---

6. *Tougher Times – Tender Hearts*, homily by Archbishop Diarmuid Martin, Archbishop of Dublin and Primate of Ireland, St Vincent de Paul Dublin Regional Conference, Croke Park, 8 November 2008.

7. *Octogesima Adveniens*, Apostolic Letter of Paul VI, 14 May 1971. This marked the eightieth anniversary of *Rerum Novarum*.

Sociological research gives further pointers. For example, in *The Spirit Level,* Richard Wilkinson and Kate Pickett show how almost every modern social and environmental problem – ill-health, lack of community life, violence, drugs, obesity, mental illness, long working hours, big prison populations – are more likely to occur in a less equal society. They contend that more unequal societies are bad for almost everyone – the well-off as well as the poor.[8]

## On the ground

As Rory, Alan and Conor got older and gave up playing games like 'going to meetings', they gained fresh insights into their father's activities. Alan remembers accompanying his father to a city flats complex. 'The local SVP visitation conference had stopped going in because so many of them had been robbed,' explains Alan. 'Dad respected their decision but didn't think it was right that families were denied Vincent de Paul support, so he took it upon himself to do the visitation and he brought along his teenage son for company. For me it was a novelty, to be in the blocks and in the individual flats. My memory is that he gave out food vouchers and, at Easter, there was a huge bag of Easter eggs,' says Alan.

His sons also recall occasional visits to particular projects. They remember the 'Treble R' training workshop where prisoners who where due to be released availed of work preparation programmes. Noel had a warm spot in his heart for the Candle Community Trust project in Ballyfermot where he served as a board member. This project, which continues to this day, was founded by a Dominican nun, Sr Caoimhín Ní Uallacháin, in the 1970s to support young men in the area, initially in arts and crafts and later in a wide variety of activities. Noel always operated

---

8. R. G. Wilkinson, and K. Pickett, *The Spirit Level: Why More Equal Societies Always Do Better,* London: Allan Lane, 2009, p. 232.

a strict code of ethics and was keen not to take advantage of his positions in any way. The only case – other than getting the tickets for Mother Teresa's visit – that any family member can cite involved the workshop in Mountjoy Prison. When a favourite family teddy bear got badly torn, Noel brought Teddy to the workshop to be stitched up.

As Noel's sons recall various humorous incidents, they also mention a house fire in 1983. Fortunately, nobody was at home at the time but the damage was extensive. Jim Guider, at that stage living in Tallaght, came to the rescue and the Clear family spent the next few weeks as Jim's guests while the Tyrconnell Road house was renovated.

## Echoes of Ozanam

Kieran Murphy, who was Director of Operations at the SVP headquarters in Dublin when Noel was national president, sees parallels between Noel's story and that of SVP founder Fréderic Ozanam.

Kieran suggests that these two men – and many others before and since – were struggling with three big questions. The first goes something like: *I see people around me who are poor, in need of food, shelter, support; how do I respond?* The basic human and Christian response can often be to give support such as money, shelter, a listening ear. This prompts a second question: *Why are these people poor?* We need to look beyond the immediate circumstances to the causes of people's poverty, to their life stories, to the opportunities they have enjoyed or not, perhaps to the way society is organised and structured, analysing forces that seem to condemn some people to a life of poverty from birth. For Kieran, the third, critical and personal question is: *What do I really believe in and how might these beliefs impact on my behaviour?* As he sees it, both Fréderic Ozanam and Noel Clear shared a deep belief in the common humanity of all people, in the fundamental connectedness between people. This positive disposition to all people, no matter what their background or position, was linked with a strong sense of God in their lives. They believed in a God who was asking them to show his love through action with, and on behalf of, the most vulnerable.

# Chapter 16
## Frustration in the Probation Service

As far back as April 1968 there were rumblings that all was not well at Noel's workplace. Well before the term 'whistleblower' became a buzzword, an explosive column appeared in *The Irish Times*.[1] Headed 'Our Hopelessly Inadequate Probation Service,' a 'Social Sort of Column' by Eileen O'Brien was based on an interview with a 'young woman who has just left the Dublin probation service in utter despondency.' The key opening words were 'frustration', 'disillusion' and 'dismay.'

The former probation officer complained that she was not properly trained for this work and she decried the lack of suitable facilities for youngsters who came before the courts. She singled out, 'an awful lot of children coming into court [who] have no criminal tendencies at all.' Shipping them off to Daingean and Letterfrack introduced them to crime. For others, being sent away from home for failing to attend school was 'inhumanly cruel' and could lead to 'untold suffering'. With responsibility for boys under fourteen and women and girls of all ages in an area that

---

1. *The Irish Times*, 22 April 1968, p. 12.

stretched across Drimnagh, Crumlin and Kimmage to Dalkey, this probation officer 'was not even provided with a car', no clerical assistance and little supervision. She compared the situation in Dublin with the much better resourced service in Northern Ireland where she had previously worked as a welfare officer.

At that time, probation work outside Dublin depended on volunteers from the St Vincent de Paul Society and the Legion of Mary, as McNally's history[2] shows. In *The Irish Times* article, the former probation officer is quoted as saying: 'They are marvellous organisations, for certain work, but this is ludicrous – of course, it is the cheap way.' She identified the commonest problems encountered as 'poverty, lack of communication between husband and wife, too many children so that the mother was so run down that she was unable to carry on and a lack of discipline because fathers were always out of the house and left everything to the mother.'

She suggests that with 'a proper probation service', the exploitation of young people in prostitution and so-called 'delinquency' could be reduced and that such a service could 'save a tremendous amount of suffering in the future'.

A week later, in Dáil Éireann,[3] the Minister for Justice Micheál Ó Móráin, stated: 'From what I have seen, I am not satisfied with the service but the main weakness, as I see it, is the overall inspiration or organisation of what is there. That was the complaint made to me'. A few months later he announced a 'detailed investigation of the existing probation and after-care service with a view to any necessary improvement'.[4]

---

2. McNally, 2009.

3. Dáil Éireann, Vol. 234, 30 April 1968.

4. Dáil Éireann, Vol. 238, 18 February, 1969.

The report was never published[5] but, according to various people, was unusually frank in its criticisms of the service's shortcomings, including poor working conditions, employee disaffection and resistance to Department of Justice intervention. According to Gerry McNally, the unpublished report 'has proved to be, without doubt, the pivotal and most critically important point in kick-starting the development of the probation service to what it has become.' In May 1970, Minister Desmond O'Malley told the Dáil, 'I am satisfied that the service is inadequate and that it needs to be expanded considerably and thoroughly re-organised.'[6]

O'Malley's proposals also suggested building on the close co-operation between the Department of Justice and voluntary groups. At that time, two Legion of Mary presidia, the SVP conferences of St Philip Neri in Dublin and St Dominic in Cork (both Catholic) and the Protestant Discharged Prisoners Aid Association had been working with prisoners, supporting them on release, complementing the work of the probation service. A new organisation, PACE (Prisoners' Aid through Community Effort), was set up in 1969 with hostel premises established at Priorswood House in Coolock, thanks to Dublin Corporation. Subsequently, the partnership model grew further. McNally[7] observes that a range of dedicated services were provided including 'training, education, addiction treatment, employment support and accommodation for offenders expanded in partnership with community-based groups using private not-for-profit companies with charitable status.'

---

5. Mc Nally quotes O Móráin's successor as Minister for Justice, Desmond O'Malley as saying that the report was an 'internal departmental report', 'not intended for publication and was written on the assumption that it would not be published. It would be contrary to established practice to publish a report prepared in these circumstances.' (McNally 2009, p. 190)

6. McNally, 2009, p. 193.

7. McNally 2009, p. 195.

Amid this late 1960s turmoil, Noel's feelings were mixed. He shared his colleagues' frustration brought about by heavy workloads, limited supports and poor morale. He was restless and considered changing jobs. Working within the Department of Justice structure was turning out to be less satisfying than he had expected. He was still living at home. His brother Seán, now married to Jean and settled in Galway, was enjoying life and work in the west. Jerry O'Sullivan had found his niche as a Legion envoy in South America.[8] Keogh Square was being demolished and while the youth club was thriving, a chapter of Noel's life was about to conclude. He began reading the jobs pages and sent off a few applications. They came to nothing and he let the matter rest. Transfer within the civil service was not considered because the probation service is what is known as a 'departmental grade', meaning specific to a particular department, in Noel's case, justice. This structure added to a sense of separateness, even isolation.

At the same time, Noel was excited about the changes taking place. New staff, usually with university qualifications, brought a fresh energy and confidence to the service. Study visits to Sheffield in England fired his imagination. Liaison with other statutory and voluntary agencies added variety to the work. Then, in 1971, Noel – along with Martin Tansey and Kay Kinsella – was promoted to the position of senior welfare officer. New responsibilities included monitoring and supporting colleagues. In August 1972, Martin Tansey was appointed principal welfare officer and head of the welfare service, a position he held until he retired in 2002.

Staff numbers grew rapidly, from eight in 1970 to thirty-one two years later. By 1984 the probation and welfare service

8. On 30 April 2015, *The Irish Catholic* published an account of Jerry O'Sullivan's activities in South America. This included his being awarded a knighthood in the Order of St. Gregory in 2005. It can be accessed at *https://is.gd/jerryosull*

employed two hundred and five people.[9] McNally[10] attributes the growth in personnel to an increased prison population and the development of community service.[11] Requests from the courts for reports on offenders from probation and welfare officers doubled between 1984 and 1989. Tom Gilmore remembers Noel's enthusiasm as national co-ordinator of community service orders. 'It was pioneering work and was supported by legislation,' remarks Tom. 'Nobody in Ireland had ever worked in this area before. Noel was an excellent boss. He wasn't a micro-manager.' Community service was close to Noel's heart, adds Tom, partly because it resonated with his youth work experience. 'We both felt that, like in youth work, you had more scope to make decisions to follow what was in the best interests of the individuals we were dealing with,' he says.

'Noel's youth work background also created some tensions in his role in the probation and welfare service,' continues Tom. 'Noel was very focused on reaching out to vulnerable young people. Government departments are very driven by parliamentary questions, ministerial profiling and that sort of thing. As high-risk clients, young offenders are always going to make the official mindset nervous. So, you can get a fortress mentality that avoids risk-taking.'

Tom accepts that Noel was also a very loyal civil servant, respecting departmental procedures as well as those in positions of authority, a realist on a tightrope. 'Perhaps because of the hierarchical nature of the department, Noel was too deferential

---

9. McNally, p. 197.

10. Ibid., p. 198.

11. According to the probation service website, 'Community Service is an order made by a court as an alternative to imprisonment. If a person is sentenced to a Community Service Order they will have to do unpaid work in the community until the Order is satisfactorily completed. A Community Service Order can be made for a maximum of two hundred and forty hours and a minimum of forty hours and it has to be completed within twelve months.'

to those "above". I think, in retrospect, he knew this and used the lesson to good effect when he became SVP President, avoiding pomp and ceremony and reaching out to everyone,' adds Tom. Others echo the contrast between Noel's caution with the probation and welfare service and his willingness to push boundaries in the SVP.

## A darker side

Importantly, the criminal population changed during Noel's working life, remarks Tom. 'When he began, most convicted offenders could be described as "ordinary Joe Soaps",' quite similar to the kids he knew through the youth club. In the 1970s, a majority were serving relatively short sentences – twelve months was a long sentence then – for crimes such as breaking into houses, car theft and so on. Many young lads in trouble with the law in their late teens and early twenties often settled down when they met a girl and sort of grew out of it. Murders were infrequent. By the time of Noel's retirement, however, the proportion of more serious criminals had increased. When the drug problem took a dangerous grip on our society in the 1980s, a lot of things changed,' says Tom.

'Noel's initial views were fairly straightforward,' continues Tom. 'TLC (tender loving care) went a long way. I remember Noel often saying: "There's good in the worst" or "Sure, he's not a bad lad". Community service worked well for such guys as there was a good likelihood of improved behaviour. The rise of drugs, gangs and guns led to a growing realisation that more specialist services and treatments were needed. Different approaches were also needed as more sex-offenders were convicted and imprisoned. Noel didn't find any of that easy,' Tom adds.

'He viewed people as basically decent. Coming face to face with someone who rapes children or who orders or carries out gratuitous violence, including contract killings, challenges this view.'

Another former colleague remarks that, although in a senior position, Noel was quick to recognise the expertise of younger colleagues. 'He didn't harp on his seniority. He hadn't a big ego. He was genuinely interested in what was best for the individual so he would refer clients to whoever he thought had the most expertise. He was able to recognise what he didn't know and that other people might do a better job, say with sex offenders or in areas like cognitive behavioural therapy or risk assessment,' he says.

### Stengths and limitations

Younger colleagues also came to see Noel as a 'go-to' person. According to Tom Gilmore, 'Even though some regarded Noel as old fashioned, they still admired him. He was always a good guy to talk to. He knew how to listen. He had a very encouraging manner even though he had limited power.' McNally has described management within the service as, '... cautious, increasingly exercising control and centralising decision-making and authority in the office of the principal welfare officer. Contact with the department was through the principal welfare officer, and little was delegated apart from management of direct casework with offenders and liaison with local courts and local prison management.'[12]

McNally's commentary tends to confirm the limited power Noel had, despite a lofty title. He writes, 'In practice the Assistant Principal Probation and Welfare Officer post in the early years was largely a "super" Senior Probation Officer, responsible for service delivery, liaison and some limited governance in their regions. Though structures had changed, the underlying systems

---

12. Ibid, p. 201.

and management practice remained highly centralised.'[13] Noel did not enjoy this regime and was known to refer to himself, in a self-mocking way, as 'The Minister for Tables and Chairs'.

However, he put his distinctive mark on the role. 'I always saw Noel as the human face of the service,' recalls a former colleague. 'I liked his management style, management by walking around, putting an arm on your shoulder, offering words of encouragement. I'd say of the people at the top, Noel was the least untrusted. He was a natural reconciler, a conflict resolver, a peacemaker, maybe more a leader than a manager. For me he was a role model of how not to become cynical'.

Tom Gilmore identifies Noel's decisiveness as another distinguishing trait. 'His mind was never too complicated,' says Tom. 'That is not to say he didn't think. A lot of us can work a simple thing into a complicated thing. Noel could see angles quickly, weigh up a 49 per cent to 51 per cent situation, be simple without being simplistic.'

Anna Rynn, who joined the Probation and Welfare Service in the mid-1970s, having previously worked in England, remembers Noel as a 'people person'. 'He had great humanity and was very much in touch with people on the ground, both those on probation and those working in the service,' she says. She also remembers him as 'an incredibly hard worker', conscientiously doing his job in the probation service and fitting in SVP work at lunchtime and after work. Anna recalls: 'If you asked, "How are you, Noel?", invariably the responses was: "Struggling like the poor farmer," but always said with a smile.' She adds, 'when someone in the office was about to get married, Noel was usually called on to say a few words and to make the gift presentation. He'd always state: "I'm a great advocate of marriage." He meant that as he and Anne had such a lovely family,' says Anna, a close family friend.

---

13. Ibid., p. 201.

Some interviewees noted that the Department of Justice was slow to provide management training for the expanding service and it was trade unions that responded most imaginatively. McNally notes, 'After 1981, when the pay and conditions of probation officers were linked to the common professional scales in the civil service, policy and practice issues became the primary interest of IPCS, UPTCS and later IMPACT, as the probation officers' union. The union played an important role in developing policy documents and pamphlets, lobbying on penal policy issues and hosting conferences in the absence of other probation-specific public discussion fora.'[14]

## The end of an era

Noel's Dad, Jack, drove his final bus journey in 1973, having reached the retirement age of sixty-five. Retirement was greatly enlivened with the company of Noel, Anne, Rory and Alan. Life's simple pleasures included a pint of stout in The Black Lion, trips to the bookmakers and watching snooker and horseracing on the television. 'He was good to us,' remembers Alan, 'one of his favourite treats for us was Jellytot sweets.' Noel often accompanied Jack to the pub and to the bookies. Occasionally the two of them ventured to watch live horseracing, especially in the Phoenix Park.

Jack, gifted in so many ways, continued to do odd jobs around the house. However, breathing difficulties had been an ongoing issue for a long time. Shortly before Christmas 1979, Jack collapsed and was rushed to Jervis Street Hospital. He died a few days later, on 15 December. Jack's passing marked the end of an era, especially for Tony, Seán and Noel.

---

14. Ibid., p. 209.

On the road again. Twins Seán and Noel preparing for their 1959 cycling tour of Ireland.

Seán, Noel and Tony.

The family in 1962. Left to right: Seán, Úna, Jack, Tony and Noel.

A busload of St Vincent's Boys' Club members heading for Clonakilty, 1961.

St Vincent's club leaders in Knockadoon, Co Cork, 1968 left to right: John Walsh, Noel Clear, Gerry Jeffers, John O'Flaherty, Tony Lawlor, Brendan Comerford, Brendan Byrne (at front, kneeling), Colbert Byrne, Terry Kelly, Tom Gilmore, Brendan Kinsella and Jim Guider.

The original founders of St Vincent's Club, Jerry O'Sullivan and Noel, in 1994 during one of Jerry's visits from Venezuela.

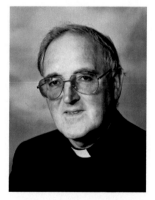

Fr Brian Power, photographed during the mid-1980s.

Top: Anne and Noel, 1972.
Bottom: Noel and Anne, in the SVP Holiday
Centre, Ballybunion, Co Kerry in 2002 at a
party to mark the end of Noel's six years as SVP
national president.

Noel speaking at the launch of the SVP annual report, 2001.

Columba Faulkner, former national secretary and Noel plant a pot of heather from
Ireland on the grave of Lonan Murphy in Lourdes, France, 1997.
Lonan Murphy was a former SVP national president who died in Lourdes in 1947.
He was forty years of age.

At the former home of St Vincent de Paul, near Dax, France. Left to right, Fr Frank Mullan CM, Frank Casey and Noel.

At an international SVP meeting in Fatima, Portugal, 1999, left to right: Anne Clear, Mary Toole, Gabriel Fay, Columba Faulkner and Noel

Mother Teresa of Kolkata visiting Dublin in 1993; picture includes Noel and Lord Mayor Gay Mitchell.

Noel speaking at Knock Shrine in September 1997 following the beatification of Frederic Ozanam. In the foreground is the oak, from Dax, that Noel planted and which continues to flourish.

Noel and SVP conference members visiting one of the SOS homes for pre-school AIDS orphans in Serowe, Botswana in April 2002.

Malawi's SVP president, Patrick Namanja, in his village of Thyolo with Noel as pillion passenger, in the year 2002.

Noel welcomes President Mary McAleese to SVP Holiday Home, Ballybunion Co. Kerry.

The Clear Family at the Lord Mayor Awards in the Mansion House, Dublin in 2006 when Noel was posthumously awarded the Lord Mayor Award, by Lord Mayor Catherine Byrne. Left to right: Alan, Anne, Rory and Conor.

# Chapter 17
## Turbulence and Disappointment

The early 1980s were a time of mixed fortunes for Noel. Family life was good for himself and Anne. Rory, Alan and the newest arrival, Conor, born in 1981, were thriving. Workplace realities involved frustration and satisfaction. However, St Vincent's youth club was heading for dramatic changes which caused much grief.

At work, spearheading community service orders was fulfilling. 'He really got his teeth into that project,' remembers Anne. Having always favoured alternatives to prison, Noel was now actively involved in rolling out a practical scheme. Real differences were being made. His leadership of colleagues also became more confident and assured.

Housed in new premises, St Vincent's club was thriving. Noel had good reason to feel that the work Jerry O'Sullivan and himself had begun two decades earlier was bearing new fruit. Never one to rest on his laurels, Noel continued to focus on how best to respond to community challenges. In March 1981, in the final issue of *The Link*, Noel reviews aspects of the magazine's twenty-year history, noting that at one stage circulation reached one thousand copies per month.[1] A trenchant article on vandalism in Inchicore dismisses attempts to blame recent incidents including car theft, window breaking and the burning of one of the priest's cars on 'teenagers coming from other areas.' Identifying 'a hard core of young people who are involved in stealing, vandalising and glue-sniffing,' Noel turns the issue back on the community asking, 'Who is prepared to take any initiative in giving these young people a new challenge in their lives?' Later, that question was to take a sharper turn.

## Inclusion-exclusion

In 1972, St Michael's became an Oblate parish with Fr Aidan O'Connor as the new parish priest and Frs Jim Hertford and Jimmy Nolan as curates. Noel had regretted the departure of his friend Fr Brian Power from St Michael's to Bray but, in time, would have reason to regret further the change in parish administration.

While deeply embedded within the parish, the SVP conference running St Vincent's had enjoyed a lot of autonomy. The group had always seen itself as focused on the marginalised, highly conscious of the legacy of the Keogh Square years. Members had a deep empathy with outsiders and underdogs. By the mid-1970s the club had a fine premises and young people from other parts of the parish got involved in activities including holidays, gymnastics and music groups. Noel feared that the needs of young people in the new St Michael's Estate were being neglected. Clashing viewpoints on priorities for the club led to tension and uncertainty. Furthermore, the St Vincent's leaders, while more

---

1. Always keen to acknowledge the contributions of others, Noel mentions Jimmy Ronan, Brian Dunphy, Brendan Kinsella, Brendan Comerford, Gay McGrath, John Walsh, Jim Guider, Terry Kelly, Anne Clear, John Flaherty, Bill Fitzpatrick, Catherine Kelly, Maire Moore, Seán Darcy, Ken Clarke, Jimmy Clarke, Michael 'Dicey' Reilly, Ann O'Brien, Jerry O'Sullivan, Tom Gilmore, Gerry Jeffers, Vincent Collins, John Geoghegan, Michael Browne, Paul Meehan, Noel Kelly, Tony Brocken, Stephen Clarke and the Ennis twins.

experienced, were also older with greater responsibilities in their lives. Volunteering in this club was especially demanding. The need for new recruits was urgent and, overall, the challenges of running a youth centre through voluntary effort became clear.

Fire in a local community hall brought further pressure on the club's facilities. In a critical move, the parish proposed that the management and administration of St Vincent's Youth Centre be transferred from the SVP to the parish authorities. A parish newsletter in October 1981 noted that 'The youth centre is one of the finest buildings of its type in the city. It is a tremendous base for community building. Moreover, it has become very clear that only the community working together could make a success of such a big building utilising it to its full potential.'[2]

Noel felt that the centre's original purpose was being discarded. He was angry, believing that his years of dedicated service were being disrespected, that the most deprived young people were being rejected. Noel and his colleagues issued a statement that noted, 'The conference regrets the present proposal to change the management of the centre, which came as a surprise. The main thrust of the SVP has always been with the disadvantaged members of the community. The conference identified closely with that objective over the years.' Those close to him remember that time as a low point for Noel; he felt alienated from many people in Inchicore and it took him time to recover from this episode.

### Distanced

With friends, Noel was frank about how these events made him feel distanced from the Church. His regular attendance at services in the two Inchicore churches faltered. On Sundays, he took off on his bicycle in search of other churches. According to Anne,

2. Subsequently, a twenty-two person committee from the four areas of the parish was formed and the term youth centre was replaced by community centre. (St Michael's Parish Newsletter, 8 November 1981)

part of his reasoning for going to Mass to the Augustinian parish in John's Lane, the Capuchins in Church Street or the Passionists in Mount Argus was that he didn't know the priests and wouldn't be distracted and could concentrate on the Mass.

With priests whom he knew, Noel discussed the youth club transfer and the bigger questions it raised. He felt conflicted in a Church he had identified with strongly. As a child of the 1940s and 1950s, Noel's spirituality was deeply personal. Always distrustful of outward show, Noel believed that actions spoke louder than words. For him Christianity was a practice. Additionally, as his brother Seán observes, fear was a major dimension in the religious upbringing of the time, especially fear of rule-breaking and of its possible eternal consequences. The possibility of dying in the state of mortal sin and being condemned to eternal hell-fire had a stark effect. For the impressionable child in Frank O'Connor's short story 'First Confession' the teacher's strategy was to talk 'of hell. She may have mentioned the other place as well, but that could only have been by accident, for hell had the first place in her heart'. It was difficult to escape the darker shadows of that inheritance.

Aware of the Vatican Council's attempt to restate the Christian message in more positive terms, Noel found solace in the new teaching, especially as he forged a spirituality in tune with his empathic identification with marginalised people. He weighed up the positives and negatives and remained an active Catholic.

Those turbulent years were also tiring. Alan recalls a time when he had pestered Noel to bring him to the cinema. 'It was a film called *BMX Bandits* and I was very keen to see it because I had a BMX bike at the time. I was probably eight or nine years of age. Anyway, he took me to a cinema in Rathmines. I don't remember much about the film but I do remember that he slept right through the whole thing.'

By way of balance, Alan also mentions that, as teenagers, a highlight for Rory and himself was meeting the Irish team for the 1988 European Soccer Championships. 'Dad knew someone involved in Finnstown House in Lucan where the team were based before they went to Germany. The place was closed to the public but Dad was able to get us in. We met the team and got photographs with the players,' he says. Those pictures with Jack Charlton, Paul McGrath, Kevin Moran and other teammates remain precious.

# Chapter 18
## Leading SVP in Dublin

'I'd like to meet Mother Teresa,' said Anne to her husband when news broke that the famous Albanian nun was coming to Dublin in May 1993.[1] By now Noel was President of Dublin Regional Council of the SVP, succeeding Bill Cleary in 1990. During her event-packed visit to the city, Mother Teresa of Calcutta (Kolkata) had requested to meet marginalised people as well as those who worked with them. Another Inchicore man, Gay Mitchell, was Lord Mayor at the time and central to the visit which included Mother Teresa being given the freedom of the city in an open-air ceremony.

Noel had known Gay Mitchell a long time and when the latter became Lord Mayor of Dublin in 1993, Noel arranged a meeting between him and the Dublin Regional Council of SVP to inform him of 'some of the poverty issues facing the people we serve.' Not

---

1. This was not her first visit to Dublin. Born Agnes Gonxha Bojaxhiu in 1910 to an Albanian family living in Skopje, Macedonia, she came to Dublin in 1928 to join the Loreto Sisters Convent in Rathfarnham. A few months later she was sent to India, completed her novitiate and was finally professed as a Loreto Sister in 1937. Mother Teresa founded a new congregation the Missionaries of Charity, to work with 'the poorest of the poor', in 1950.

unsurprisingly, Gay Mitchell involved Noel in the preparations for Mother Teresa's visit.

Anne says, 'Initially Noel was reluctant because he was very strict about protocols being followed and never wanted to take advantage of his position. Then he arrived home with two tickets for an early morning gathering in the Mansion House.' Conor had just made his Confirmation. 'I remember walking down Grafton Street, over to the Mansion House to a breakfast supplied by Feargal Quinn of Superquinn,' he recalls. Mother Teresa spoke briefly to the invited guests, flanked by the Lord Mayor and Noel. 'It was an honour to meet her, shake her hand and say hello,' recalls Anne.

'A few days later we met her again at an event in Donore Avenue,' continues Conor. 'The place was packed and there was a lot of pushing. I got close and said, "Hi" and I think she said, "Bless you my child". I asked her to bless the Rosary beads I'd got for my Confirmation. She did, putting her hand on my head.'

On 2 June 1993, outside Dublin's Mansion House, in front of thousands, the City Council presented Mother Teresa with the freedom of the city.[2] During her short visit to Dublin, the eighty-two-year-old nun also visited President Mary Robinson.

Subsequently, Noel used the visit to sharpen SVP focus on its core mission. In the autumn 1994 issue of *Society News* he wrote:

> In our work we must always be seeking to find the poorest of the poor. In every parish there are people in desperate

---

2. Since Isaac Butt was made the first freeman in 1876, less than one hundred people have been awarded this honour. Mother Teresa was joining the company of the likes of Hugh Lane, John McCormack, George Bernard Shaw, Chester Beatty, John F Kennedy, Eamon de Valera, Pope John Paul II, Maureen Potter and Nelson Mandela. Subsequent recipients have included Jack Charlton, Bill Clinton, the members of U2, Mikhael Gorbachev, Aung San Suu Kyi, Bob Geldof, Brian O'Driscoll and Peter McVerry SJ.

need of the help of the Society ... the problems will differ from area to area and will not always be financial. Caring for the elderly and the lonely, offering a relief service for carers and developing a befriending service for the disabled ... are increasing needs ... What can the Society do to help small groups of local vandals and give them some direction in their lives in responding to the challenge of Mother Teresa; no work of charity will be foreign to the Society, no matter how unsavoury or unpopular it may be?

Gay Mitchell remembers Noel as 'a very genuine, humble man'. The former Lord Mayor who was a TD in Dáil Éireann for twenty-six years and subsequently represented Dublin as a member of the European Parliament for a decade, continues, 'I admired Noel hugely. He had a great *grá* for the underdog. I especially admire the way he plodded along, working quietly, not seeking attention for himself, initially in St Vincent's club in Keogh Square, then with the SVP Council of Youth Clubs and later as national president of the Society. He was a born diplomat, constant in his loyalty to Vincent de Paul values and to the less fortunate. Noel had deep convictions without ever being in your face. Of course, he wasn't perfect but there was a saintliness about him that was admirable.'

Noel's involvement in Mother Teresa's high profile visit contrasts sharply with the multiplicity of meetings he attended as leader of the SVP in Dublin, often in the evenings, in parish halls and presbyteries. Fellow volunteers remember Noel's readiness to offer support and encouragement. 'He had great energy and he was so willing, never complaining about the workload,' remembers Columba Faulkner, a former national secretary of the SVP. She remembers how Noel frequently cycled over from the probation and welfare offices in Smithfield to the SVP offices, first in Nicholas Street and then in New Cabra Road, during his lunchtime, dealt with correspondence – a world before e-mail – returned to work and later that evening attended one or two meetings.

As president of the Dublin region, Noel was keen to bring a greater urgency and efficiency to the SVP. He felt frustration when council meetings were indecisive and bureaucratic. He wanted action on many fronts – tackling poverty, moneylending, unemployment, offering home management courses. He was annoyed when important items surfaced randomly at meetings, so promoted the idea of discussion documents being circulated in advance. This led to a more structured and effective approach to a range of policies. In addition, Noel became more skilled at managing an agenda and getting decisions made.

### 'Wardrobes of the poor'

From the earliest days of the SVP in Ireland, providing recycled clothes was a key service, sometimes referred to as 'wardrobes of the poor'. The idea is simple and straightforward: those who, for whatever reason, no longer want clothes, footwear, furniture and so on, donate them to the SVP and in turn SVP volunteers re-distribute these to those who need them. Today, people are familiar with the network of SVP shops across the country, examples of the charity shop phenomenon. It was not always so. Until the 1990s, the SVP stored second-hand clothes in warehouse-like re-cycling centres, called 'Salvage Bureaus'. Conferences gave people tickets and recipients made their way to places like Ozanam House in Dublin's Mountjoy Square and rooted through bundles of material. 'It is not very dignified,' Noel often remarked. The SVP set about shifting the emphasis. As Dublin regional president, Noel set up a shops council in 1991. A key decision was to move to bright, modern and attractive premises. This led to the opening of a series of high street shops trading initially as 'Fred's Fashions', later as 'Vincent's'. It was a spectacularly successful decision.

Michael Wall, then president of the Rathdown SVP region, has been central to this project. He had spearheaded the opening of a shop in Dundrum in 1989. 'I liked the name "Fred's Fashions" as it was a reference to Fréderic Ozanam, the SVP founder,' says Michael. With shops opening in Finglas, Tallaght and Crumlin, Michael approached Noel with the idea of a shops council and suggested employing a full-time administrator. 'He reacted so well,' recalls Michael. 'That's it, Michael, he said, we'll run with the idea. And he did. He was always such a positive, joyful committed Vincentian. He trusted people. I'm grateful for the trust he put in me.'

Michael, with a marketing background in Bord na Móna and St John of God Hospital, became the first full-time administrator of the shops, a role he filled for ten years. Michael's own SVP journey dates back to his days as a schoolboy in Coláiste Mhuire when, as a sixteen year old in 1953, he became a volunteer. He was subsequently involved in setting up the first hospital visitation conference in Dublin, as well as the conference in his own parish of Meadowbrook. Michael also played a central role in the society acquiring the premises in Seán McDermott Street that houses the spacious SVP national headquarters. In addition, Michael was a founder member, in 1966, of Dundrum Credit Union.

Nowadays, the network of shops is a sophisticated, dignified operation. New and second-hand goods are available to all at affordable prices and some much-needed income is generated for the SVP. Local conferences provide people with Vincent's Gift Tokens which can be used in any Vincent's shop.

## Gateway

While his responsibilities now extended to all aspects of SVP work in the capital, youth work activities still held a special place in Noel's heart. He was especially delighted when the Council of Youth Clubs won a 'Better Ireland' award in 1990. This was for the Gateway Project in Edenmore Youth Club, Raheny and carried a grant of £25,000. The Gateway Project represented a new way of working with young people who were out of work. It involved adventure sports, rock climbing, community service as well as close individual support.

## Work is the key

Noel was pleased when, in 1992, the Irish Catholic Bishops' Conference issued a pastoral letter, *Work is the Key*.[3] The subtitle was 'Towards an economy that needs everyone'. The authors are quick to acknowledge that, 'As bishops, we have no expert advice on how jobs might be created'. However, they assert that: 'High unemployment is causing suffering to an extent that is wholly unacceptable. More can be done to reduce it, and more must be done.' While striving to avoid aligning themselves with any particular ideology, the bishops remark that 'wasteful expenditure is far more conspicuous among the well-to-do than among people who are poor.' *Work is the Key* invited creative responses at grassroots level within the Church. The bishops wrote: 'we urge every parish and Christian Community to show creativity and determination in bringing people together from every walk of life to forge a truly inclusive community where the rights of unemployed people are fully respected.'

Noel and the SVP in Dublin were already deeply engaged with job-related initiatives. It was encouraging that the bishops

---

3. A popular edition of the bishops' pastoral letter was published by Veritas in 1996; 'Work is the Key: Towards an Economy that Needs Everyone'.

prioritised the need to tackle unemployment. Noel favoured community efforts to bring about jobs. SVP conferences had begun to support people with viable business ideas. In the early 1990s the SVP supported the Action Tallaght Enterprise Centre in Killinarden. When handing over the money, Noel was forthright in asserting the value of supporting local initiatives. In Tallaght, a panel of experts assessed the projects and, depending on viability, recommended small grants and gave practical advice. Noel knew that some projects would fail to take root but emphasised the need to nurture hope, people's sense of value and self-worth.[4]

His deep respect for human dignity also led Noel to champion social employment schemes, forerunners of community employment schemes. He knew the difference to a person's self-esteem and daily life that can come from a job contributing to local health, education or environmental projects. In practice, the bishops' call for action at parish level was often met through the local SVP Conference.

## Difficult and contentious issues

In December 1992, events unfolded that led Noel to initiate a review of SVP services for the homeless. The bodies of two homeless people, Pauline Leonard and Danny Lyons, were found in a derelict site in Blackhall Place. They had died of exposure and hypothermia. Revisiting these tragedies nearly a quarter of a century later, resonances with more recent events are disturbing. When, in December 2014, Jonathan Corrie, a homeless forty-three year-old Kilkenny man died within shouting distance of the national parliament, there was a sense of outrage and shame. Back in 1992, urgent meetings were held, high level committees put in place, extra bed places provided until the issue slipped down the

---

4. The SVP Bulletin, Winter 1999-2000 carries an article by Fintan Tallon, 'Has the Society a Future in the New Millennium?' that recounts some SVP initiatives in job creation and community revitalisation.

news agenda. There are not many votes in homelessness. While the SVP, the Simon Community and other groups continued to respond to the challenges, Noel knew serious policy change was needed.

In 1995, in an editorial, *The Irish Times* recalled the 1992 tragedy, acknowledged the persistence of the homeless problem and noted that, 'The voluntary organisations know the problems on the ground and the harsh reality'. The newspaper supported a proposal by Alice Leahy of Trust that a forum be set up whereby voluntary organisations would work with programme managers of each health board – this was an era before the HSE (Health Service Executive) – pooling resources and making practical solutions.

A depressing feature of these 1992 and 2014 stories is that homelessness in the capital has worsened. In August 2016, Pat Doyle, Chief Executive of the Peter McVerry Trust, declared, 'the problem of homelessness is now out of control'. He told RTÉ's radio programme *Morning Ireland* there were six thousand five hundred people in emergency accommodation, including the highest ever number of children. A comparative study[5] found that, in Ireland, there is an increasing 'feminisation of homelessness' with more than 40 per cent of homeless people being women. In other parts of Europe, typically women make up between 20 and 30 per cent of the homeless population.

## Bigger questions

Noel, the volunteer and the civil servant, grappled with homelessness and related issues. He thought deeply about the relationship between voluntary organisations and state services. Would some services be better provided by state agencies? How

---

5. P. Mayock and J. Bretherton (Editors) *Women's Homelessness in Europe*, London: Palgrave Macmillan, 2016.

should a charity best deploy its limited resources? Should charities always accept government grants? Does the state find it more convenient to allow charities to supply services it should provide to people as their right? Since the foundation of the Irish State, successive governments have facilitated voluntary organisations – most notably Church groups – to establish and provide health, education and social welfare services. Sometimes, the state abdicated its responsibilities, in terms of oversights, funding and partnership, with all sorts of unfortunate consequences.

His unique experiences led to Noel being invited to contribute to numerous groups, often dealing with difficult issues that were very close to his heart. For example, in 1995 he found himself on a sentence review group within the Department of Justice, chaired by Mary Kotsonouris, a district justice.[6]

## One-Hundred-and-Fiftieth Anniversary

Noel's time as president of Dublin Regional Council of the SVP – he was re-elected for a second term in 1993 – coincided with the one-hundred-and-fiftieth anniversary of the society's arrival in Ireland. The initial meeting took place on 16 December 1844 in Charles Street West in the parish of St Michan's, Halston Street. Redmund Peter O'Carroll, a lawyer and friend of the then Archbishop Daniel Murray, was the first conference president and among those present were Dr Thomas Willis and John O'Hagan, a Young Irelander.

The anniversary was marked by Mass in St Michan's Church in Halston Street on 4 December 1994. The chief celebrant was Bishop Eamonn Walsh and Fr John Wall delivered a lively homily. Despite there being much to celebrate after one hundred and fifty

---

6. Other members included Charles Smith, Dermot Walsh, Gisella White, Martin Tansey, Seán Alyward, Henry Mitchell and John Kenny. Dáil Éireann Debates, 3 October 1995, Vol. 456, No. 3, p 117. Written reply by Minister for Justice, Nora Owen TD.

years, Noel was never going to rest easy on past achievements. He reminded his fellow volunteers that the society should respond to 'the new needs and changing social conditions in Ireland'. He added, 'this demands a greater sense of creativity from members in helping people to help themselves, and an openness to the Spirit of God working within our Society and in society in general.' This emphasis – respecting SVP's tradition of charity and justice but recognising that changed circumstances demand new initiatives – was a defining feature of Noel's leadership in the society.

### Fundraising

Despite the weighty social problems that rested on Noel's shoulders as SVP leader in Dublin, he remained cheerful and good-humoured. He often spoke about how energised he was by people's generosity to the society. He was supportive of imaginative and traditional fundraising efforts. Occasionally, the family joined Noel at such events and Rory, Alan and Conor remember being in Croke Park in 1991 for the football and hurling games between Dublin and the Blue Stars[7] from which the SVP benefitted.

Noel's leadership of the SVP in Dublin both strengthened the organisation and increased his national profile. This was to lead to even greater responsibilities and challenges.

---

7. Similar to the GAA All Stars, the Dublin Blue Stars are annual *Evening Herald* awards for the best player in each given football and hurling position. The annual challenges games between Dublin and the Blue Stars provides a showcase opportunity for emerging county players.

# Chapter 19
## On the National Stage

Noel was elected SVP national president in 1996 and immediately tackled his new role with enthusiasm and vigour. That autumn, he indicated his intention to focus on four main SVP themes: the Christian dimension; support and friendship; promoting self-sufficiency; and working for social justice. He wanted to build on the society's distinguished history in Ireland since 1844, applying core principles to the particular circumstances of 1996.

From a young age, Noel had taken to heart the words of Jesus: 'For I was hungry and you gave me food; I was thirsty and you gave me drink; I was a stranger and you made me welcome; naked and you clothed me, sick and you took care of me, I was in prison and you visited me' (Mt 25:35-39). He saw this as a defining statement for Christians. Noel believed he would be judged on how he responded to these challenges, aware that 'in so far as you did this to one of the least of these brothers of mine, you did it to me.' For Noel, a love of Jesus Christ manifested itself in a love of other human beings. Being a Christian was about being a good human being, committed to the common good of all people.

Noel often highlighted the work of conferences that visited those in psychiatric wards and in prisons, some of whom struggled to conduct a rational conversation or had committed crimes that angered the public. Noel greatly valued work where: 'in the spirit of the Gospel the members of the society continue their visitation work from one week to another, bridging the gap with each individual visited between the reality of the world outside and the situation in which they find themselves trapped.'[1]

## Social Policy Group

Early in 1997 Noel decided to put in place a national advisory group on social policy. John Monaghan was a key member of the initial group and went on to be a leading SVP voice in the media. In the early 1990s, at a members' day in St Patrick's College, Drumcondra Noel had been impressed by John's presentation and chairing of the subsequent discussion. John, who grew up in Drimnagh, was Professor of Mechanical Engineering in Trinity College and a very active member of the SVP conference in Leixlip, Co Kildare. 'I had heard about Noel, mainly through Seamus McGivern in the Leixlip Conference who knew him from regional meetings,' explains John, 'but I didn't know him. I was happy to accept the invitation to join a national social policy group.'

The core idea of the social policy group was that a blend of active members, employed staff and others with particular expertise would attempt to give voice to issues arising from the day-to-day encounters SVP members had with people in need. The thinking was that such an overview might identify the impact of public policies on poverty and inequality. Thus, the SVP could advocate with government departments and political parties for more just policies. It wasn't as if Noel was 'inventing'

---

1. *SVP Bulletin*, 22.3 Autumn 1996, p. 4.

social policy work; advocacy with government departments had always been a strong aspect of SVP work in Ireland[2]. Noel felt that the changing circumstances of the mid-1990s demanded new initiatives.

Noel's opinion was that the SVP was not adequately regarded as 'the voice of the poor'. He said, 'the members of the society have vast first-hand experience of how people are affected by social exclusion.' He believed that the national council had 'a responsibility to harness that knowledge and use it to attempt to effect changes in the structures of society.' Hence a social policy group.

'A major task every year is to make a pre-budget submission,' explains John. The group addressed a wide range of issues. A 2002 report, for example, prioritised educational disadvantage, income adequacy and rural poverty. A consistent focus has been on identifying the root causes of poverty and social injustices and, in solidarity with poor and disadvantaged people, advocating for the changes needed to create a more just and caring society.

The SVP social policy group has been effective in shifting the society's public profile. SVP's work of charity in alleviating people's pain and suffering through handouts is now seen as complemented by action for justice. Noel encouraged volunteer members to engage with the media. 'He also wanted the social policy group to give voice to people's lived experience of being poor in today's Ireland. I found myself doing a lot of these media interviews,' explains John. 'All the time the focus was on being able to refer back to what SVP members were finding when

---

2. One dramatic illustration of the SVP's relationship with government departments occurred in 1979 when post office workers went on strike. Minister for Health and Social Welfare Charles Haughey approached the society and asked members to ensure that social welfare recipients got their entitlements. SVP volunteers distributed welfare payments to seventy thousand recipients during the strike. See *The Irish Times* 27 March, 29 March, 11 June 1979.

they visited people in difficulties. I wanted to be able to say with confidence – this is what is happening to lone parents, this is what is going on for people in education, early school leavers for example, here is what's happening with the number of people on housing waiting lists and so on. It was important to back up what we were saying with evidence.'

Initially, John found it daunting to react to 'a microphone stuck under your nose from Martina Fitzgerald or Vivienne Traynor' but he quickly got on top of things. 'We didn't go out seeking publicity,' John adds. Journalists and others came to the society looking for comments on issues. Many recognised John as a credible, authentic voice on issues such as poverty, inequality, injustice. He is especially good at showing how relatively simple changes in policy can make big differences to people's quality of life. In 2012, after more than a decade as a voice of the society, John decided to play a less public role. 'I am not comfortable with the same person in a voluntary organisation always being the spokesperson,' he explains. He did continue as a national vice-president for social justice and advocacy.

### Staffing decisions

Among the key, and at times, controversial decisions, Noel made was to employ additional professional staff, both to streamline the SVP's internal workings and to sharpen its voice in public fora. One of his first actions as president of the SVP Dublin region had been to employ Liam O'Dwyer as a regional administrator to succeed Charlie Gallagher, a much-loved figure in head office. Liam and Noel worked closely and well together. Liam had little doubt about the urgent need for the SVP to modernise. 'I remember the first day I walked into the office. I was handed a ledger, a neatly, handwritten document. It was very old fashioned. Not much had changed since the 1950s or 1960s,' says Liam of a time when computers were starting to revolutionise office practices. Later, when Noel was national president, Liam became SVP national co-ordinator. This decision ruffled some feathers as it was a clear signal that Noel wanted to push the reform agenda further.

Some believe that Noel's decision to employ a social policy officer was particularly inspired. However, not everyone was happy. Prior to taking up her job in the SVP, Mary Murphy had worked for the Irish National Organisation for the Unemployed. She brought to the role a deep appreciation of the nitty-gritty of how poverty disadvantages individuals and families. Not only was Mary passionately committed to working to right wrongs, she could articulate complex unjust and unequal situations succinctly, coherently and credibly. Producers of radio and television programmes valued Mary as a contributor and social commentator. It was a powerful mixture. Media organisations quickly recognised her effectiveness and she became a regular guest on primetime radio and television programmes.

Liam O'Dwyer contends that Mary's professionalism and advocacy skills, combined with the leadership and on-the-ground experience of John Monaghan as volunteer chairman of the social policy group, were especially effective. 'Together, they helped, particularly through their media performances, to re-position the society as a credible voice of people in poor and marginalised situations,' says Liam. Noel, who never regretted the decision to employ Mary, frequently had to take phone calls from irate SVP members who believed the social policy officer brought the society too far into the political arena as she trenchantly critiqued aspects of child benefit measures, housing policies and, crucially, annual budgets. Noel, the good listener, pointed out to the callers that the society's concern was always a compassionate one and that if government policies were hurting poorer people there was an obligation to say so. Sometimes he was given a good hearing, though on occasions the phone was slammed down. Noel remarked that sometimes the ire seemed to arise because an individual SVP member's own political party of preference had been criticised.

Mary subsequently became a lecturer in politics in the Department of Sociology at Maynooth University and continues to write and comment insightfully on social justice matters. John-Mark McCafferty replaced Mary as national social policy officer, continuing the tradition of well-researched analysis, articulate advocacy for the voiceless and media-friendly communications.

**Much travelled**

Columba Faulkner, SVP national secretary when Noel became president, is just one of many who marveled at his willingness to accept invitations to speak at conferences, workshops and meetings. For example, within a few weeks in 1998, Noel visited Brú Mhuire, North Great George's Street; a youth festival in Artane; a youth group in Wesley House, Leeson Park, Dublin; turned the first sod for a housing development in Cavan; handed over a cheque to SVP in Omagh, Co. Tyrone following the 1998 bombing; attended the one hundred and fiftieth anniversary celebrations of SVP in Kilkenny and numerous other meetings. 'He never went unprepared. I often researched a conference for him and he was sensitive to their issues and concerns. He would greet each person individually. He was so warm and genuine,' says Columba.

**Engaging words from former SVP member Mary McAleese**

Noel was particularly pleased that the President of Ireland, Mary McAleese, in her first year in office, accepted an invitation to address SVP conference presidents in Drumcondra in 1998.

My connections with the Society of St Vincent de Paul go back to my schooldays in Belfast when I set up the society in St Dominic's – my school,' she told the gathering. 'As a member of its National Youth Council in the late 1960s I made many contacts and friends from Dublin to Derry, all of whom, thankfully, are still close friends to this day. I suppose you could say that it was while I was on the youth council that I first learnt how to build bridges – a skill for which I have had much use since – and for which I am extremely grateful. But my gratitude goes beyond that – because my first training in TV was courtesy of St. Vincent de Paul, which very generously sponsored me on a communications course in 1970 in Dublin. That training was to be the start of a successful and enjoyable career in broadcasting. So, I have a lot to be thankful to the society for – and I am more than happy to acknowledge that debt here.

Picking up one of Noel's persistent themes, President McAleese spoke about changes in society since she was a child. She warned against the 'veneer of progress and gain' masking a world of want and deprivation.

This new manifestation of poverty – the poverty of prosperity – is a task that the society faces today, in communities throughout Ireland that find themselves trapped in cycles of disadvantage that become increasingly difficult to escape from. While the problem remains the same, the changes in Irish society mean that the problem must be addressed in a different way, in a way that reflects the new structures that exist and the new challenges that individual and communities face as we approach the new millennium.

'Justice is a fixed star,' she declared, 'it can be seen from different angles, but justice itself remains unchanged.'[3] The President commended the work of the SVP, noting that its past success had been 'in its ability to address the changing circumstances in which it operates and that has been facilitated by a membership which has been willing and eager to make the adjustments that are needed.' This was indeed music to Noel's ears as McAleese was echoing key themes of his presidency. 'That ability to critique and review is what will keep the society focused on its mission – through support and friendship to promote self-sufficiency and self-worth and to work for social justice,' she said. Noel also used this occasion to acknowledge his wife Anne's role as his supporter and companion on his journey. Anne, on behalf of the SVP, presented President McAleese with a floral 'thank you'.

## From the ground up

John Monaghan cites the *From the Ground Up* initiative as a further example of Noel's modernising of the SVP. The policy stresses the importance of SVP members actively listening to how poverty impacts on people and was driven by the social policy group. 'Quickly, we had to accept that what we were getting was being filtered, even distorted. We needed to get as close to people's lived experience as possible,' recalls John.

> We began to assemble credible stories about accommodation, about educational assessments, about how individual families were caught in poverty traps. The FTGU initiative is about gathering such stories, having members share them and giving voice to the emerging patterns. Phone calls to other

---

3. Here the president was referring to a quotation from Fréderic Ozanam. The Ozanam quote is: 'Justice is a fixed star which human societies try to follow from their uncertain orbits. It can be seen from different points of view, but justice itself remains unchanged.'

SVP members across the country means a picture on a particular issue can be built up quite quickly.

## Stability

One of the many important phone calls Noel made when he was elected national president was to Philip Furlong whom he had known through the Council of Youth Clubs. 'I was surprised and delighted to get a call from Noel inviting me to become the national treasurer. Being part of the National Council was a great honour,' says Philip, now retired from the Department of Finance. As national treasurer between 1996 and 2002, Philip, as well as overseeing financial matters, saw Noel up close, as he engaged in a process of improving practice at the SVP and responding to emerging challenges in an ever-evolving Ireland. 'Noel took the role very seriously. Of course, there were differences of opinion but, to be honest, I would find it impossible to say a bad word about Noel. The sheer goodness of the guy kept coming through,' says Philip. He adds that Frank Casey, a long-time SVP volunteer and former CEO of the ICC (Industrial Credit Corporation) was especially supportive of Noel.

## Proud father

Striking a balance between the demands of the workplace, his unpaid SVP leadership and his family was a continual challenge. Noel valued and enjoyed the times with Anne and their three boys. He took great pride in the various achievement of Rory, Alan and Conor. One highlight Noel liked to recall was the passing out ceremony in the Garda College in Templemore, Co. Tipperary in July 1998 when the family watched Alan become a member of An Garda Síochána.

# Chapter 20
## The Moderniser

By the time he became national president, Noel's extensive experience within the SVP had given him unique insights into the organisation's strengths and weaknesses. Rooted in parishes across the country, he knew how well positioned SVP conferences were to provide quick and effective relief from the harsher effects of poverty. At a time when the reputations of many established organisations were taking a battering, he knew the positive regard many Irish people had for the SVP. This needed to be maintained. Noel also valued the tradition of volunteering that had sustained the organisation for more than a century and a half.

Noel was a realist as he sought to modernise the SVP. He recognised and respected the rich tradition, stretching back to 1844, rooted in volunteers engaging in family visitations. But times were changing and the society needed to respond. Paul Cummins says, 'Noel didn't want to disrupt the close bond members had with the people they served but he believed the society could be better organised, make more use of its considerable but finite resources.' Paul, an active volunteer in his local conference, had a professional background as an accountant with PriceWaterhouseCooper (PwC) and was aware how optimum allocation of resources could lead to organisational effectiveness. Noel had invited Paul onto the national council.

'Noel and myself had many disagreements, but, looking back, he had a very clear vision, trying to move things forward, to steer the society's resources – money and members – in new directions,' recalls Paul.

## Coherence

As a voluntary organisation expands, the sheer logistics of scale usually require paid and administrative support staff. Noel knew this was another sensitive topic. The SVP ran hostels, holiday homes, shops and various special works and had a national head office. According to Paul, 'in the late 1990s there were probably over six hundred employees on the SVP books, some part-time, some full-time. Like everyone else, SVP has to comply with employment and tax legislation. Noel wanted this done properly. We created a committee to deal with HR [Human Relations] in a more organised way. Noel wanted staff matters to be dealt with sensitively and properly. He worried that some volunteers appeared to have a haughty approach to paid staff.' For Noel, a key goal was respectful working relationships between volunteers and paid staff, with no 'second-class citizens'.

John Monaghan confirms the ongoing challenges facing an organisation with so many local branches. He says, 'A big positive is that a local conference can be proactive, agile at doing things, quick to respond to challenges on the ground. Big organisations move slowly.' However, from the perspective of the national management group – of which John has been a member – the scenario of hundreds of independent republics is a nightmare. 'A single employer – SVP – makes sense. We try to coordinate employment contracts, pay scales, entitlements, PAYE, PRSI but also advise on purchase of property or other big spending. We watch when debts are incurred.'

Paul Cummins often accompanied Noel on visits to regions around the country and they had lengthy discussions about the SVP's organisational structure. 'I often said to him that the SVP was a bit like the GAA or Fianna Fáil, with cells all over the country. One cell doesn't necessarily know what another is doing. You can't run an organisation like that without some national scrutiny or accountability. It's like a franchise. Everyone has to play by the rules of the franchise. Noel sought to bring a national coherence to the SVP. That can be a thankless task. That's where Noel's clear vision was a great help,' says Paul.

## Confusion

Paul adds that when Noel initiated discussions on modernisation at the national council, differing views on poverty and the role of the society emerged. 'Originally, the SVP was born in Ireland as a response to destitution at a time when people had no food, no shoes. For the past thirty or forty years in Ireland, there has been very little destitution but far more poverty. There was confusion in some members' minds between destitution and poverty. Poverty is when you are missing the various elements you need to develop as a human being within the society you live in,' explains Paul. 'We needed to ask if some of the aid we were giving to the poor was patronising and too financially orientated. We were trying to develop the concept that there were a lot of other needs that we were not addressing. For example, mothers in poor households can be easily ignored. Some members saw it as a luxury if they got money for a hairdo or an opportunity for a holiday. But these people are the lynchpins of their families. Noel was very supportive of expanding our understanding of poverty,' continues Paul.

'There is a contrast between the child of a parent who is addicted to drugs or serving a prison sentence with one who, say, has a university degree. One child is poor and the other is probably not. How should the SVP attempt to respond to these deficits? We were good at responding to financial deficits; that's relatively simple. Noel and myself discussed at length how to deal with the more complicated, subtle forms of poverty,' says Paul.

Paul and Noel debated and argued about many topics: pre-budget submissions and whether they were too reliant on statistics and relative income; absolute and relative poverty; priorities for conferences; local autonomy for conferences; the role of the national president. The latter was especially contentious, says Paul. 'Noel wanted to keep in touch with local conferences, staying grounded, still doing home visitations and listening to the voice of the poor. I wanted him to be more strategic.'

### Critique

For Noel, and others, a continual axis of tension was: how critical should the SVP be of government policies, especially as support for the society comes from all walks of Irish life. Paul says, 'Noel was clever in that he didn't want to politicise the society. He was at times outspoken but I would have liked more agitation especially about abuses in government spending, of not prioritising the needs of the poor.' He adds, 'the role of national president is a thankless one. Few understand what they do. Making sure things don't go off the rails in a big voluntary organisation is not easy. You don't get much credit for keeping the ship steady. We have been fortunate in having presidents who were good at keeping stability.'

Recalling their road journeys together, Paul adds: 'He was a great companion. He used to tell me stories from his work, from his youth club activities and about his family. I got a strong sense of his attachment to family. He loved trips to London with Anne and Conor for the musicals. Some stories were hilarious. You knew the way he'd tell stories about "this poor devil" and "that poor devil" that he was very compassionate towards people in difficulties. He used to sing a lot when driving. Occasionally we would drop into a bookies to place a small bet on the horses.' Paul continues:

> At times, Noel was exasperating. He was very good at seeking advice and then making up his own mind. He was his own man. I remember an invitation to a meeting with the archbishop [of Dublin], relating to collecting outside churches. I was full of fire and brimstone, and angry at the clerical Church. The diocese said only five [members] from the SVP could attend. I said we should bring as many as we like, arguing that the laity *is* the Church. We are the Church. We should go to the meeting as equals. I wanted to go and bang the table. Noel made sure that I was not one of the five. He was very clever like that. Shrewd.

### Are we doing enough?

'Noel's dedication and commitment were outstanding,' says Larry Tuomey, a long-standing senior figure in the SVP who was recently appointed Treasurer General of the International Council. 'Our paths first crossed sometime in the 1980s when Noel invited me to talk to the youth clubs council about Vincentian values. Later, when he was Dublin president, I became vice-president. Then when he became national president in 1996, I became regional president in Dublin. We were on the national council together from 1996 to 2002. He was very hard-working. I often remember the rest of us would be going home after a meeting, say at eight o'clock and he would be heading off to an area meeting or some other SVP activity. I have a very clear memory of him, as national president, asking "Are we doing enough? Should we be doing more? What things should we be doing?"' recalls Larry. Did that annoy some people? 'Probably,' he smiles, 'some people like a quiet life.' Larry adds that his preferred definition of the SVP comes from the first revision of the original 1835 Rule which was agreed after the Second Vatican Council in the 1960s. It states that:

> The source of the Vincentian vocation is both human and divine. It is the anguish experienced in seeing the suffering of another human being; the spontaneous reaction of sympathy, even fury, which surges in the presence of injustices undergone by our brothers and sisters in humanity. It is also the attitude of the Christian, living in the hope of the Resurrection, the bearer of a message of hope to those who suffer.

Paul Cummins adds: 'Noel's commitment to the work of the SVP was huge. He didn't have a big ego. It wasn't about him. It was about tackling poverty and inequality. He wasn't in the society to make friends. He rubbed some people up the wrong way, especially when he insisted that correct procedures needed to be followed. He was very conscious of public trust in the SVP and strove to safeguard that.'

As Larry Tuomey sees it, Noel came into national office at a critical time for the society. In 1995, a group chaired by Gerry Martin had worked on a mission statement. 'It focused on three strands of our work: support and friendship; help towards self-sufficiency; and a concern for justice. Noel really took these seriously,' explains Larry. 'This gave a very clear direction to our work. Noel got people on board. It gave the work a fresh framework and a new impetus'. The justice strand was contentious for some. 'When an SVP person was on television, for example, some members saw them as straying into the political arena and were against that. But justice and politics are so interconnected you couldn't avoid it. It was even more sensitive if we were perceived as having a party political bias. You have to watch that,' Larry adds.

Those three strands of SVP work have evolved since the mid-nineteenth century. Indeed, the history of SVP in Ireland shows it responding well to changing circumstances. Circumstances during Noel's leadership – the start of the so-called Celtic Tiger years – changed and, arguably, the need to campaign and lobby at policy level was more urgent than ever. In an insightful reflection on fifty years as an SVP member, Liam Fitzpatrick, a former treasurer general, has written:

Fifty years ago, the SVP was not as involved in advocacy as it is now. In the current climate, being a voice for the poor is a very important part of our activities. Without a well-informed and professional input on their behalf, there is a grave danger that the interests of the less well-off will be neglected, and the SVP has sufficient standing that its views carry weight. Our exhortations do not always yield the desired results but, without our voice, it can be safely assumed that the assistance provided to the poor by the national government would be considerably less than it is[1].

Larry Tuomey summarises Noel's contribution thus: 'I think he changed the direction of the society. It had been a bit comfortable, a bit complacent. With the assistance of the new mission statement, Noel gave the SVP a new direction that emphasised justice.

1. L. Fitzpatrick 'Fifty Years a Vincentian: A Personal Journey' in *The Society of St Vincent de Paul in Ireland; 170 Years of Fighting Poverty* edited by Bill Lawlor and Joe Dalton, Dublin: New Island, 2014.

Despite an apparent calm, focused exterior, Noel found tensions and disagreements uncomfortable, even stressful. His sense of responsibility for the workings of the overall SVP in Ireland combined with his own high standards and expectations became, at times, a heavy burden.

## Council meetings

National Council meetings could be difficult. The society's mid-1990s restatement of its mission attempts to move beyond a paternalistic perspective. Relatively wealthier people quietly and discreetly giving money to less well-off people through the SVP is a strong tradition but needed to be more nuanced. For Noel, the idea of 'solidarity' became a powerful one; for others, it was contentious. For some, the term triggered images of events in Poland from the late 1970s, particularly the *Solidarnoc* trade union movement led by electrician Lech Wałęsa. Was this too 'political', a tacit challenge to established authority? Within the tradition of Catholic social teaching, solidarity is about the ties that bind all human beings together. None of us is an isolated individual; our well-being is inextricably linked with the well-being of others. No matter how materially prosperous we may feel, we are diminished as humans when we live in a world characterised by glaring inequalities. Back in the 1960s[2], Pope Paul VI stated that: 'There is no progress towards the complete development of women and men without the simultaneous development of all humanity in the spirit of solidarity'. Pope John Paul II stated that:

> ... solidarity must be present whenever it is called for by the social degrading of the subject of work, by exploitation of the workers, and by the growing areas of poverty and even

2. In the encyclical *Populorum Progressio*.

hunger. The Church is firmly committed to this cause, for she considers it her mission, her service, a proof of her fidelity to Christ, so that she can truly be the 'Church of the poor'.[3]

At its most basic, the key idea in solidarity is that, as humans, we are all brothers and sisters, equal in dignity.[4] Occasionally Noel's frustration with the pace of progress was palpable. According to John Monaghan:

Noel was very fortunate in having Columba as National Secretary at his side. She knew the right bits of information to feed to him. She was a great support to him. I've often seen her at meetings leaning over very quietly, saying things like take it easy or don't let them get to you. Some of the people on the national council didn't really want to be there. Even regional presidents were rooted in their local conferences, areas and regions. The national perspective didn't always interest them, they saw themselves as representatives of their region. They found it hard to think beyond their region, to see the national picture.

## Always positive

Despite tensions, Paul Cummins believes that Noel succeeded in many ways in modernising the SVP, partly because of his personality. 'Even if certain members did not agree with his

---

3. Pope John Paul II, Encyclical Letter *Laborem Exercens*, 14 September 1981.

4. In St Paul's first letter to the Corinthians, he uses the analogy of the human body. 'Just as a human body, though it is made of many parts, is a single unit because all these parts, though many, make one body so it is with Christ. In the one spirit we were all baptised, Jews as well as Greeks, slaves as well as citizens, and one spirit was given to us all to drink.' (1 Cor 12:12) The letter continues by asserting that the weaker parts are the most indispensable ones, and that 'You together are Christ's body; but each of you is a different part of it' (1 Cor 12:27).

approach, he continued to be well-liked and appreciated. Noel was one of those people who emits positive ions. You just have to like them, everybody does. That was a great asset,' he says.

When, in the early days of the social policy group, criticisms from other SVP members surfaced, support from the national president was critically important. John Monaghan says, 'One of the great things about Noel was that once we explained the issue that we were going to raise publicly, he was supportive. His disposition was: Go for it and I will support you. Noel was not a micro-manager. That meant we had real freedom. That trust made it easier to express clearly how badly people were suffering.'

In time, internal opposition to the social justice work diminished. John believes this was 'because any time we went out we were backed up by the facts'. John believes strongly in the value of data to support SVP members' vision and commitment. 'For better or for worse, we had to get as close as we could to the people we were supporting. You are better to tell stories, paint pen portraits; people will listen more to stories than they will to statistics,' he says.

Some tensions Noel encountered arose from change itself. As in many organisations, the familiar usually offers more comfort than the unknown. 'The way we've always done things' has an in-built attraction, especially if the organisation is regarded as 'successful' in its mission. Consistently and calmly, Noel focussed on the big picture, wishing the collective energy and resources of SVP members be channelled more effectively in responding to poverty and inequality. He emphasised the bond of shared core values rather than focussing on differences.

John Monaghan adds that Noel's idealism was also tempered by a pragmatic realism. 'I'd say that Noel was a very wise man, very circumspect. He drew on all his experiences of interacting with people. He used to say that every time he met someone he learned something. Noel was a good listener; he would enter in a conversation when meeting someone for the first time without too many prejudices or expectations. That's a great quality in a leader.'

It's important to underline that when Noel emphasised social justice in the SVP, he knew he was continuing a proud tradition. He had great regard for long serving members who, week in, week out, in conferences around the country, discreetly eased the burdens of poverty, marginalisation and inequality. He was very conscious of the contributions by his predecessors as national presidents, people like Bill and Bob Cashman, Cormac O' Brion, Don Mahony, Frank Cox and Bill Cleary. What was perhaps unique to Noel's presidency were the unprecedented social and economic changes emerging in Ireland, what subsequently became known as the 'Celtic Tiger'. New manifestations of traditional challenges demanded new responses.

# Chapter 21
## To Paris for a Beatification

A particularly memorable event during Noel's time as SVP President was the beatification, in Paris in August 1997, of Fréderic Ozanam, the principal founder of the society. Noel led an Irish delegation of about two hundred people including his wife Anne and their son Conor.

The title 'Blessed', given at beatification, indicates official Church recognition that a deceased person lived a life of heroic virtue, now enjoys a new vision of God and has the capacity to intercede on behalf of people who request that intercession in prayer. The beatification by Pope John Paul II was a lively, colourful, celebratory occasion for SVP members from across the globe. *The Irish Times* reported that, 'The Pope drew cheers from the crowd when he recalled that he had joined his local St Vincent de Paul group when he was a student in pre-war Poland'.

Noel's friend and SVP international vice-president Gerry Martin recalled how the sight of so many television cameras indicated that the beatification was indeed an event of international significance. Gerry found himself seated next to a great grandniece of Ozanam and later met the great grandson and great granddaughter of the very first president of the SVP, Emmanuel Bailly.

Gerry also remembered how, the night before the beatification, the Irish delegation hosted a memorable meal in a Chinese restaurant near the headquarters of the Vincentian Fathers. Delegates from England, Scotland, Wales, Canada, the United States, Germany, France and Nigeria mingled with the Irish. Gerry said Noel warmly welcomed the guests, many of whom noted that the Irish SVP group included two archbishops, Seán Brady of Armagh and Desmond Connell of Dublin, and a bishop, James McLoughlin of Galway.

At the beatification in Notre-Dame Cathedral, Pope John Paul II recalled how Ozanam knew it was not enough to speak about charity and the Church's mission in the world. 'This needed to be translated through an effective commitment by Christians in the service of the poor,' he said. 'Love for the most wretched and for those whom no-one cares about was at the heart of the life and concerns of Fréderic Ozanam'.

The international head of the SVP, César Augusto Nunes Viana from Portugal, spoke about the need for the SVP to adapt to the times we live in, '... an era of great social, cultural and moral crisis, the result of an economical crisis and of technological development...' He reminded listeners that Ozanam and his fellow founders acted 'with a sense of dynamism, hope in the future, a generous acceptance of risks and a creative imagination. They relied on adaptability to new situations and so we must adapt to new situations ahead also'. Noel found the events in Paris inspirational, with many signs encouraging him to push forward in adapting the SVP to suit Ireland's changing conditions.

Conor took part in some World Youth Day events which coincided with the beatification. 'I was an awkward teenager at the time but it was enjoyable. There was a good vibe. I did get to meet a lot of people my own age. I also remember Dad had a guidebook, *Pauper's Paris,* and we did get to see a lot of the city,' he says.

'Overall,' says Anne, 'it was a very memorable and special occasion. Beforehand, I decided to buy a mantilla to wear on my head inside the cathedral. I tried loads of shops in Dublin, places like Clery's and Arnotts, but there wasn't one to be found. I did buy a little hat but, in the end, it wasn't needed,' she laughs. 'Then on the day of the beatification, we arrived late for the ceremony. Joe Little of RTÉ had interviewed Noel and that was fine but there were a lot of traffic restrictions in place. Our taxi took ages to get us to the cathedral. When we got there our reserved seats had been taken. Fortunately, there was a youth group from Dublin, I think it was Edenmore, and they gave us their seats. We were grateful for that. It was wonderful that the cathedral was full of Vincentians. It was a great boost for the SVP,' she says.

### Irish celebration

Following the Paris event, the Irish Vincentian family organised its own celebration at Knock Shrine, Co. Mayo on 13 September 1997. One thousand five hundred people turned up, including members of the Daughters of Charity, the Vincentian Fathers and the SVP. Numerous colourful banners resplendent in the sunshine indicated the SVP's national character. Welcoming visitors to the basilica, the Archbishop of Tuam, Michael Neary, spoke of how poverty can be concealed in an economic boom. He saw SVP members as dealing with deprivation 'which may be concealed behind closed doors that only opened to the special nature of the society, which demanded confidentiality of all its members in dealing with the problems they encountered amongst the deprived'.

Social justice campaigner Sr Stanislaus Kennedy also addressed the pilgrims, stating that the SVP 'stood in the gap' between the rich and poor in an Ireland where the rising tide of affluence had only been a 'rising tide of exclusion' for the poor. 'As Christians,' she declared, 'we cannot stand idly by or remain indifferent. We must work relentlessly for a radical redistribution of our resources in favour of the poor.'

Noel also spoke, welcoming various strands of the Vincentian family and thanking dozens of people. Noel also reminded those present of the SVP's core ethos. 'Inspired by our founder, Fréderic Ozanam and our Patron, St Vincent de Paul, we seek to respond to the call every Christian receives to bring the love of Christ to those we serve in the spirit of the Gospel message: "I was hungry and you gave me to eat".' He recalled the recent deaths of Princess Diana and Mother Teresa of Calcutta and saw a common thread as the gift of love of fellow men and women. 'In a world where life is not always treasured, where the poor and the lonely are often rejected and isolated, where many young people are exploited and become the victims of drug addiction, broken marriages, suicide and so many other modern phenomena, the example of the love of St Vincent de Paul and Fréderic Ozanam, Princess Diana and Mother Teresa was never more relevant than it is today,' said Noel.

## Oak tree

The day concluded with Noel planting a small oak tree, re-dedicating the SVP to the ideals of Fréderic Ozanam. The tree had been grown from an acorn brought from the birthplace of St Vincent de Paul, near Dax in south-west France. In Vincent's home village, now renamed St Vincent de Paul, opposite a reconstruction of Vincent's family home, there is an oak tree said to be over eight hundred years old; Vincent often rested under its shade. In planting the tree, Noel stated: 'We pledge to ensure the continuation of Fréderic's legacy to us by inviting many more people to join with us in living the Gospel the Vincentian way.'

Today, visitors to Knock will notice a granite plaque beside the oak tree. It reads: 'This tree was planted on 13 September 1997 by Mr Noel Clear, National President, Society of St Vincent de Paul, to commemorate the beatification of Fréderic Ozanam, founder of St Vincent de Paul'. Coincidentally, Pauline Joyce from Dunmore Co. Galway, mother of Rory's wife Kathyrn, played an important role in getting this plaque erected.

## Congratulatory letters

Following Ozanam's beatification, the national president received many congratulatory letters. These give some indication of how the SVP was regarded at that time.

President Mary Robinson wrote: 'As a force to harness the goodwill and caring concern which exists within communities, the Society of St Vincent de Paul ranks among the most successful.' She added, 'One of the great strengths of the society is the fact that it is community based – comprising members of the community who work voluntarily to help others in the community who are disadvantaged or in need.' President Robinson regarded Ozanam's beatification as 'appropriate recognition of his caring vision and of the dedication of members, past and present, who have made their personal commitment to community service'.

Taoiseach Bertie Ahern also wrote to Noel. He noted that, 'For over one hundred and fifty years, the society has played a leading role in caring for the most disadvantaged members of the community. The self-effacing person-to-person contact, which is the hallmark of the society's work, has won the support and admiration of the entire community.'

In his letter, Archbishop of Armagh, Seán Brady, recalled how delighted he was to have been at the 'wonderful occasion' in Paris. 'Blessed Fréderic Ozanam is an inspiration to all of us,' he wrote. 'He devoted his great intellectual ability to the explanation and defence of Christian teaching. He was ever on the lookout for occasions of serving Christ by renewing the temporal order. May his beatification suggest new ways to the Society of St Vincent de Paul of intensifying its activity.'

## Ozanam in his own words

The beatification prompted Noel and other SVP members to discover more about Fréderic Ozanam. While the context of mid-nineteenth century France differs greatly from that of modern Ireland, they were pleasantly surprised to discover the relevance of Ozanam's actions and words. Selected quotations from a souvenir bulletin give a flavour of how Ozanam saw challenges:

1. It is a matter of grave social concern whether the spirit of selfishness or the spirit of self-sacrifice will prevail, whether society is to be merely a means of exploitation for the benefit of the strong, or the consecration of each for the benefit of all, especially the weak.

2. So many have more than enough, yet want still more; so many have less than enough, but are determined to take what society refuses to give them.

3. These two classes are preparing for battle and the fight threatens to be a terrible one, the power of wealth against the power of despair.

4. No Christian may stand aside and remain indifferent. We must throw ourselves between these two armed camps. If we cannot prevent, at least we can soften the clash.

5. I ask you: let us occupy ourselves with people who have too many needs and not enough rights, who call out rightly for a greater involvement in public affairs, for guarantees of work – and who cry out against misery.

## Chapter 22
# What Should the Priorities Be?

In the late 1990s, reflection on the century and millennium about to close and speculation about the future intensified. How might the twenty-first century and the third millennium of Christianity unfold? In 1998 Noel wrote that, since its foundation, 'the unique contribution' of the SVP had been 'the person-to-person contact that members have with those who are unfortunate to be disadvantaged'. He cited Ozanam's simple model of 'bringing support and friendship to people in need, in their own homes' as a 'cornerstone,' pointing out how 'each week all over Ireland SVP members continue that tradition,' and how other society services 'focus on offering individuals practical support.'

Noel encouraged conferences to monitor the quality of visitations, ensuring that respectful, dignified human encounters were at the heart of the work. Throughout his six years as national president, Noel reiterated this message up and down the country.

## Educational disadvantage
As he travelled the country listening to members' views, Noel discovered that many volunteers shared his opinion on the importance of education in breaking the cycle of poverty in which

many families were trapped. Conferences often supported schools in practical ways: funding breakfast clubs and other simple meals, supporting supervised study and homework sessions, offering reading material to promote literacy, contributing to the cost of Junior Cert and Leaving Cert exam fees.

Early in his work in Keogh Square, Noel became convinced of the centrality of education in shaping life chances. In late 1997, he spearheaded two SVP strategic initiatives. He invited the social policy committee to map vital education issues. They produced *Priorities in Education* which formed the basis of SVP policy on educational disadvantage. The second strategy was to meet Education Minister, Micheál Martin. Noel knew that educational disadvantage was a multi-dimensional problem that needed a nationally coordinated response across the various sectors of the education system. His goal was to impress upon the minister the many links between poverty and educational provision. In April 1998, Noel, accompanied by Liam O'Dwyer from the SVP head office and myself of the social policy committee met Minister Martin.

The SVP delegation prioritised extending the *Breaking the Cycle* initiative. This scheme targeted schools with high concentrations of poverty. It provided extra-staffing, funding, in-career development and, critically, a pupil-teacher ratio of 15:1. Feedback and evaluations indicated very positive results. Noel and his colleagues also suggested reduction of class size at primary levels, particularly in schools where learning difficulties were pronounced, adequate funding for pre-schools for Traveller children and the abolition of fees for state examinations.

The Minister indicated respect for the work of the SVP and appeared keen to address issues of educational disadvantage. At times, the conversation got heated, particularly when discussing *Breaking the Cycle*. Throughout the meeting one glimpsed Noel's skill as an advocate and negotiator: he listened carefully and respectfully and remained calm, his voice at all times reasonable and patient and, with great determination, he maintained his focus on the issues.

Liam O'Dwyer remembers that Noel often remarked: 'The society is here for the long haul, so we don't want to burn bridges unnecessarily.' That is not to say he didn't share the anger and frustration being expressed by colleagues. 'I think he had a good appreciation of how different people on a delegation can play different roles,' adds Liam.

It is difficult to assess the impact of such meetings. Ministers are forever meeting delegations and deputations. Warm handshakes, lots of smiling and enthusiastic nodding don't automatically translate into policy change. As a civil servant, Noel had few illusions about this process. However, he believed strongly in the importance of SVP leaders informing policy makers of the realities that conference members were encountering. Furthermore, Noel came to see advocacy with those in powerful positions as needing to be practical, focussed and specific, rather than vague and aspirational. Through the international SVP family, he learned that opportunities for the SVP to meet government ministers face-to-face was far from commonplace. His conviction of the value of the society engaging in social analysis and advocacy deepened, seeing it as an essential complement to what members were doing at local level through home visitations and special works.

### Social Policy Manifesto
This new emphasis on social analysis and advocacy depended greatly on research. Social policy officer Mary Murphy collated various SVP documents into more focussed and coherent policies, including a *Social Policy Manifesto* in 1999. Mary travelled far

and wide, listening to members' experiences to ensure she was familiar with conferences' situations 'on the ground'. That *Social Policy Manifesto* still strikes a challenging and radical tone. Liam O'Dwyer still remembers Mary handing him a draft of the document. 'I read it and said to Mary that this is to the left of Karl Marx; the society will never buy into this,' he recalls. 'Mary suggested that I go and reread some papal encyclicals. I took her advice and it was great to be able to back up what we were saying with reference to *Pacem in Terris*[1], *Populorum Progressio*[2] and other Church documents. I think that document we produced was a very important one,' says Liam.

Mary and subsequent social policy officers turned out to be a great resource for the SVP. Members were alerted to the relevance of government policies to their work. Governments were reminded that promises made should be promises kept. Data-driven research opened up new avenues for lobbying and campaigning, ensuring that SVP voices were heard nationally. Links were established with organisations that shared some of the SVP vision.

## The Stranmillis Four

While usually calm under pressure, occasionally Noel found his patience stretched. Tom McSweeney, a long-time SVP member, remembers one such occasion. Noel and his wife Anne, and Tom and his wife Kathleen, were guests at the annual meeting of the SVP in Northern Ireland in 1999. Having checked into a hotel, Noel drove the foursome the short distance to the conference

---

1. Pope John XXIII's final encyclical letter *Pacem in Terris* (Peace on Earth), published in 1963, addresses many issues including human rights, the common good and the non-proliferation of nuclear weapons.
2. Released in 1967, Pope Paul VI's encyclical letter *Populorum Progressio* (The Development of Peoples) expresses concern for the growing inequalities in the world.

venue at Stranmillis College. That evening, following the formal proceedings, delegates and guests enjoyed a fine dinner and some excellent music by Tom Laverty in particular. 'I still have one of his CDs with songs like "Rathlin Island", "Teach Your Children" and "Forty Shades of Green",' recalls Tom. A warm, convivial atmosphere developed and all four guests enjoyed the conversation, music and *craic* with their northern hosts. 'Knowing that Noel was driving, the three of us enjoyed a few drinks and all four of us were in great form, not in any rush to get back to the hotel,' says Tom. Eventually they left, located Noel's car and headed in search of a way out of the campus. 'The gate was shut and I could see Noel was a bit put out,' continues Tom. 'We drove to another exit. Closed. Then the main exit. Also closed. We were teasing him – are you really the national president and you can't find a way out?' Apparently the security system was such that, after one am, the gates could not be re-opened. 'Noel was adamant saying, "we have to get out,"' says Tom, a glint in his eye as he relives the episode.

Anne, recalling the incident remembers Noel saying, 'If they can get out of Colditz, we can get out of here.' Spotting two large dustbins, the group decided to scale the railings. Tom, who had some knowledge of Belfast from his time there in the late 1960s as an *Irish Press* journalist and later as an RTÉ reporter, was first up and, with helping hands, made it to the other side. Anne and then Kathleen were helped over the railings, 'with decorum', adds Tom. So, with three on the outside, Noel was still stuck inside. With some difficulty, and jocose encouragement from his three companions, Noel eventually made it to the top of the railings. 'The next thing,' remembers Tom, 'some students, on their own way home from a night out, spotted us. Can I have a bit of what you're on? shouted one young chap to Noel. They were tickled by the idea of four older adults "escaping" from the college.

"Where are you off to? Can we come too?" Noel, becoming more impatient, stated firmly, "You can't. Go home.", and flagged down a taxi. The hotel was only a short walk away but Noel was keen to get there as fast as possible. The first two taxis refused to take us as a student had attached himself to Noel, shouting – "Take me with you".' The third taxi driver was more obliging and the group arrived safely at the hotel. To the suggestion of a night-cap, Noel responded, 'Didn't you have enough to drink!'

Next morning, back in the college, the story had taken on a life of its own. 'In welcoming delegates and guests, I remember the chairperson having a special welcome for 'The Stranmillis Four,' says Tom, smiling. 'We had many a good laugh over that bizarre episode. We imagined how different it might have been had the RUC[3] stumbled upon us; SVP national president, RTÉ reporter and their wives caught escaping from Stranmillis,' laughs Tom.

## Unmaterialistic

'Noel was so unmaterialistic. That's how I remember him,' recalls Bernie Hughes who has worked in the SVP head office for more than three decades.

> When I got to know him first he would arrive up at the Old Cabra Road (then SVP HQ) on his bicycle during his lunch hour. He might have six or seven handwritten A4 pages of minutes of a meeting, or a speech or his vision. I know he was often up to two in the morning writing these. I think it was his gentle manner. He was very approachable and we often had a good laugh. He had some curious expressions. He would often say: 'Can you get me this on the gogglebox?' That was how he referred to the computer. It was a very happy time when

---

3.  The Royal Ulster Constabulary was the police force in Northern Ireland until 2001 when it was replaced by the PSNI (Police Service of Northern Ireland).

he was Dublin president. He just included everybody and treated everybody the same. Even now it's quite emotional talking about him.

Bernie explains what she means by 'unmaterialistic'.

Once, we were both at a function in the Mansion House. I live on the South Circular Road, not far from Inchicore. It was a wintry night, rain and wind. Noel said he'd give me a lift. Right. Now, he'd always come to the SVP on his bike so I'd never seen the car. When I saw it, I thought 'Oh, my God', but, being polite, I got in. I think I said, 'Noel, do you really think you need a chain and a Chubb lock on this car? Anyway, he undid the lock, took off the big chain and took off. After a few minutes, I couldn't see anything through the windscreen because it was such a bad night. He didn't seem a bit concerned. I asked, 'Shall I open the window?' But the window wouldn't open. And the heater fan didn't work. As was as if nothing in the car worked, but that was Noel: material things didn't matter.

Bernie smiles and continues in a more serious vein.

For me, Noel embodied the Vincent de Paul ethos. He had a vision. He did the work. He didn't want any recognition. He was never about how it was going to benefit him. I know he was a regional president and became national president but that wasn't what it was about for him. He was there to help people, to progress social policy. That came across very strongly. He was very committed. He had seen deprivation up close.

## *Chapter 23*
# Giving of his Best

As SVP National Secretary working in the society's head office, Columba Faulkner was well placed to see the pressures national presidents face. How did Noel respond? 'Never, no matter what demands were made of him, no matter how full that little diary became, did I hear him complain. I remember when I would remark on how busy he was and how did he keep going, his reply was "he took on the task and now he was going to give it his best".'

Noel travelled up and down the country – often after a day's work – meeting members, congratulating those with long service, viewing new projects, all the time affirming volunteers in their efforts. Opening a housing project in Mullingar, acknowledging volunteers with fifty years' service in Enniscorthy, attending a regional meeting in Coleraine, then a mayoral reception in Clonmel or a national council event in Kerry were 'normal' for Noel, recalls Columba.

No matter how big the organisational issue, Noel never lost sight of the individual person. Indeed, this was one of his defining and most attractive features. Columba puts it like this: 'If Noel met you once and you shared a family story, the next time you met, he would ask about the family member. He took a genuine interest in everyone. I used to say to myself – how can one head carry such detail?'

After Noel died, Columba gained further insights into how he was a friend to so many who had lost their way. One particularly bereft man used phone Columba regularly, saying, 'Noel never judged me. I served my time and Noel was there for me when I came out. He understood me. I have no one to tell my troubles to now, to share my fears for the future. I miss him so much'.

Columba adds: 'We will never know how many there were for whom Noel provided a shoulder to cry on.' Columba also marvelled at stories she heard of Noel fighting quietly for people in danger of eviction. She remembers occasions when callers objected to the presence of neighbours with prison records and Noel's peacemaking skills were well deployed.

### Children

While as national president Noel had to attend numerous meetings and focus on 'big-picture' thinking, he never lost his awareness of how vulnerable children are to poverty. For Columba an incident from Easter Saturday 2002, illustrates this:

> I met Noel outside the office at 9.30am. We had bought two hundred Easter eggs the previous day. We loaded up the two Starlets and headed off around the city. Many of the places we visited were bed and breakfasts where Noel knew there were children who would not otherwise get an egg. Noel knew them by name. There were some who were looking forward to making their first Communion and Noel knew that their mums were worried. He assured them that the SVP would help as best it could. Promises were made to him that the eggs would remain in their boxes until the following morning. I can still see Noel smiling as he looked back at one house where we saw a lovely smiling face smeared with chocolate as its owner waved at us.

Noel's son Conor remembers a few occasions when he travelled with his father 'down the country'. 'Every SVP event was very hospitable,' he says. 'Tea and cake. You couldn't refuse the cake, or the sandwiches or the biscuits!' Conor also remembers when he ended up beside a bishop watching a rugby match. 'He was really involved, the bishop,' explains Conor. Smiling, he adds, 'It was probably good for me to hear a bishop shouting at the referee in choice language. Part of my education.'

## Strategic leadership

While Noel was a person-focused individual, some of his capacity for shrewd strategic thinking derived from his past. His former colleague Gerry McNally echoes a comment from Tom Gilmore when he says, 'there are interesting contrasts between his time in the probation service and the SVP especially the national president role. It's almost as if one was a training ground for the other. He saw the limitations of top-down management. He harnessed volunteers in the SVP very well. He empowered people to act responsibly.'

Early on in his papacy Pope Francis used a colourful and memorable phrase, suggesting priests should be 'shepherds living with the smell of the sheep'. By this he meant staying close to the marginalised in society, the poor, prisoners, the sick, those in sorrow and alone. As a leader exercising the priesthood of the laity, Noel was always close to people in need and an excellent role model for fellow Vincentians. Liam O'Dwyer remembers his capacity for forward thinking, often stating: 'We need to move away from the handout' to link charity and justice, handouts with social analysis, food vouchers with critique and advocacy'.

Noel often spoke about the faith the Irish people had in the SVP, as evidenced by the generous donations received at local and national levels. He frequently asked, 'Are we making to best use of this money to fight poverty?' He was very aware of the need for good governance at all levels in the SVP.

As a people-focussed leader, Noel knew that a great strength of the SVP was the commitment of its volunteers. He encouraged initiatives to recruit new members. His experience in the probation and welfare service also taught him that well-meaning intentions needed to be harnessed with appropriate training and education. He also recognised the power of modern communications. Traditionally, SVP volunteers had been self-effacing, often almost anonymous. Noel, essentially a private person, appreciated the opportunities to remind people of the work of the society on television, radio and in the newspapers. He was never about promoting himself, always focused on the issues, amplifying the case of the marginalised.

## Setbacks

Aware of the trust the public had in the SVP, Noel often remarked how important it was to manage donated money efficiently. He knew that, with so many people handling SVP monies, the possibility of lapses of judgement or, worse, of straightforward theft, was real. Noel was keen to strengthen the checks and balances to ensure that spending was transparent and people were accountable.

## More than a wake-up call

A major setback occurred in 1996. Sunshine House in Balbriggan, Co. Dublin had, for six decades, provided a dedicated holiday home for thousands of disadvantaged Dublin children. The initiative had multiple benefits. Children got a week's holidays by the sea with regular wholesome meals and group activities staffed by SVP volunteers. Parents appreciated the break from the intense and demanding work of child-rearing, often in cramped and inadequate conditions. The idea caught the public imagination and the annual Palm Sunday collection outside churches, accompanied by *The Advocate* newspaper, was supported generously. In 1991, a particularly large bequest to the Sunshine Fund had been invested with a reputable company. On 26 August 1996, *The Irish Times* reported that 'The Society of St Vincent de Paul last night confirmed that £185,000 which it had invested with Dublin broker, Mr Tony Taylor, had gone missing. The money had been earmarked for an indoor play centre in a home which the society uses for summer holidays for less-well-off children from the greater Dublin region.' It subsequently emerged that seventeen other accounts had also been mismanaged. Taylor fled the country. He was arrested in England three years later and subsequently received a five-year jail sentence for fraud.

This incident caused great anguish throughout the SVP. Noel and other senior figures were very distressed. However, the story didn't end there. In January 2000, the *Fingal Independent* reported the good news that the 'top investment firm Fidelity Investments' had made a donation of £150,000 to Sunshine House. Taylor had been a former master agent of Fidelity. The paper added that: 'A new indoor play centre for disadvantaged children will be built with the substantial donation.' The incident reinforced Noel's commitment to wise and prudent management of SVP finances.

**Family holidays**
If the sand dunes in Laytown were a key image from summer holidays when Noel, Seán and Tony were young, 'caravan' was a by-word for Noel's sons Rory, Alan and Conor. The family invested in a caravan in the mid-1980s. Anne recalls that, shortly after they were married, they did take one holiday in Spain but Noel was not a fan of hot weather and 'he really loved Ireland'. At first, annual holidays were in rented houses, usually for two

weeks, in West Cork or Kerry. 'I also remember one in Donegal and a lovely one in Achill. We used to pile everything into the car – bicycles, a record player as well as clothes and games,' she says.

The caravan enabled them to travel throughout Ireland and with two notable exceptions – Dungloe, Co. Donegal and west Kerry where it lashed rain all the time – they were fortunate with the weather. 'It was grand,' remembers Anne. By the 1990s, Noel was prepared to venture further afield with the caravan and there were some memorable holidays in England and Wales, including to Tenby, Aberystwyth, Yorkshire, Newcastle and Stratford-on-Avon.

Conor's memory is of an annual ritual manoeuvring the caravan out of the back garden. Rory adds, 'There's a very tight squeeze around the corner and we had to get the neighbours involved in a real community effort.' The boys' memories are laced with warm laughter as they recall incidents and accidents. 'On the one hand, there would be so much stuff packed in that you would have to remove it in order to get in. At the same time, on at least one occasion we were so organised for the ferry in Dún Laoghaire that we stayed the night before in a caravan park in Shankill,' adds Alan. 'You could eat your dinner off the floor' is a phrase his sons recall following Noel's initial reconnaissance of a caravan site, usually referencing the bathrooms or shower blocks. 'They were very well kept,' remembers Alan, in particular the Eagle Point site overlooking Bantry Bay. 'Spotless. We got off to a good start,' he says.

## Reunion

One caravan holiday was prompted by an unexpected knock on the door. A man introducing himself as Brendan Mooney and a friend of Juju Clear wondered if the Clears still lived there. Noel's aunt Julia (Juju) – Jack's only sister – had gone to England in the 1940s and contact had been lost. Brendan had a phone number and Noel called Julia, bridging a gap of nearly half a century. Unfortunately, Jack was dead at this stage. Noel arranged to meet Juju and her family in Droitwich in Worcestershire in the summer of 1994. 'That was a lovely reunion,' recalls Anne. 'Noel was so delighted to meet Juju after all those years. He was only a boy when she left. One of the sons-in-law was a hotelier and we all gathered in the gorgeous grounds of a big country house.'

## Musical tastes

From the mid-1990s, Noel, Anne and Conor began to make annual trips to London, usually after Christmas. 'That's how I developed my interest in theatre and drama,' explains Conor. '*Oliver* and *Cats* were the first. Sometimes we would see a show on a Friday and maybe a matinée on the Saturday. We stayed in a bed and breakfast named *Springfield* – they called it a hotel – run by a Cypriot woman called Vesula,' he says.

Noel loved these excursions, though his strongest musical preferences were for Irish traditional music, folk music and the showbands. According to Conor: 'Dad liked the radio, especially Donncha Ó Dúaling on *Fáilte Isteach* on a Saturday night. Often after dinner, he would go out to the kitchen to do the dishes. He had cassettes and CDs. Sonny Knowles, Daniel O'Donnell, Brendan Shine and, of course, the Bachelors. Dad loved telling us about the time the Bachelors knocked the Beatles off the top of the charts back in 1964. Out in the kitchen he'd start singing. A few occasions when I had friends over, they wondered about the racket coming from the kitchen,' he laughs. Alan adds that, 'Yes, it was mainly showband stuff but then I remember one time, maybe sometime in the early eighties, he bought this LP by Boney M with songs like "Rasputin" and "Rivers of Babylon". So, his taste wasn't that narrow'.

Noel didn't watch much television, though he did like to catch the news and, during election time, was a keen viewer. Rory recalls watching stages of the Tour de France with him, 'especially in the 1980s when Seán Kelly and Stephen Roche were big,' he says. Neither was Noel a frequent cinemagoer. He did have a great fondness for *The Quiet Man*[1]. 'He really loved that film,' recalls Conor, himself very knowledgeable about movies. 'Whenever it was on TV, usually around Christmas, we'd watch it together. And we had a video of it. I don't know how many times I viewed that as a kid; definitely his favourite film,' adding, 'We did a kind of pilgrimage to Cong one year to see the various locations, even the beach at Lettergesh. He really was a fan.'

---

1. A 1952 film, directed by John Ford, set in the west of Ireland, starring Maureen O'Hara and John Wayne.

# Chapter 24
## Working together against Poverty

Noel had a great ability to work well with others. As national president he strengthened collaboration between the SVP and other organisations. At conference, area and regional level there were projects in association with county councils, with health boards and local voluntary groups. Nationally, Noel encouraged collaboration with agencies as varied as government departments, the Combat Poverty Agency, Barnardo's, the Children's Rights Alliance, and the National Youth Council. Two examples illustrate Noel's gift for promoting partnership.

### The wider Vincentian family

As a practical response to homelessness, the three partners in the Vincentian family – the Daughters of Charity, the Vincentian Fathers and the SVP – formed the Vincentian Housing Partnership. Directors were drawn from all three 'family members', with Noel one of the SVP representatives.

This co-operation led, in the mid-1990s, to the foundation of the Vincentian Partnership for Social Justice[1]. It's a good example of how groups sharing a common vision can work together. Subsequently, the Sisters of the Holy Faith joined, explains Sr Bernadette McMahon, Director of the Partnership. Each of the four groups has a special link to the inspiration of St Vincent de Paul. 'We came together to work in more strategic ways to combat poverty and social exclusion. In those early days, Noel was very supportive of the work,' she adds. 'He encouraged, inspired and challenged us as we developed the vision statement, values and goals of the Partnership.' In time, as Noel's responsibilities increased, he lessened his engagement in the day-to-day running of the partnership. 'However, his interest and support did not diminish. He made a lasting contribution to the spirit and work of the VPSJ,' recalls Sr Bernadette. Throughout the life of the VPSJ, Noel's fellow SVP founding colleague Larry Tuomey has maintained the strong SVP link with the initiative.

Sister Bernadette, a former provincial leader of the Daughters of Charity, is a soft-spoken woman with a deep commitment to social justice. The partnership pioneered voter education workshops in Ireland. 'The intention is to encourage people in disadvantaged communities to find their voice and to use it,' says Sr Bernadette. The three-hour workshops, based on the principles of Brazilian educator Paulo Friere, are 85 per cent participation and 15 per cent information. They draw on the experiences, knowledge and wisdom within the group. Participants find them enjoyable, affirming, challenging and educational. Workshops usually have a transformative impact on the majority of participants. Sister Bernadette acknowledges that mistrust of the political system is widespread. 'Yes, people in disadvantaged communities often

---

1. The founding members of the VPSJ were Noel Clear, Fr Michael McCullough CM, Sr Bernadette McMahon, Fr Mark Noonan CM, Sr Catherine Prendergast and Larry Tuomey.

feel alienated. They ask: what's the point? Politicians only lie. They make promises. They do nothing.' However, rather than dwell on the anger, the workshops are designed to assist people to get in touch with their own power, their own capacity to shape their lives.' A telling comment from one participant on the vote.ie website states: 'I found the programme powerful and I regained my power as a citizen'.

Having listened carefully to women speaking about poverty, Sr Bernadette began to develop projects related to the practicalities of day-to-day living in poor circumstances. 'I remember one woman saying: I wish somebody would show the government what it's like to live on social welfare, on a minimum wage,' she recalls. In response, the partnership undertook a small study in 1998 and then a bigger one in 2000 entitled 'One Long Struggle'. The goal was to make available detailed information of the actual cost of a minimum standard of living. 'We look at various family models, urban and rural, identifying what you have to spend to achieve an acceptable standard of living and how much you need to earn,' she adds. The partnership has built a powerful collection of factually-based resources. The websites, justicematters.ie, budgeting.ie, misc.ie offer families, advocacy groups and government departments reliable, accessible data on the costs of basic living. The latter website, for example, provides an easy-to-use 'minimum income standard calculator'.

The partner organisations fund the partnership's office on the top floor of Ozanam House in Mountjoy Square, Dublin. State support for the various programmes and workshops has almost evaporated since the recession. At one stage there were up to sixteen workers on Community Employment (CE) schemes. Today, core staff are mainly volunteers from the partner congregations. Those who take part in workshops frequently have limited resources, and include participants from the Travelling community, family resource centres, migrant groups, homeless agencies and adult education groups, as well as recovering addicts, lone parents groups and former prisoners. 'We ask for a small charge or contribution towards the expenses of facilitating the workshops. However, for groups with little or no funding for workshops there is no charge,' explains Sr Bernadette. In 2014, the Loreto Foundation Fund provided funding for workshops in preparation for the local and EU elections.

'At present[2] there is funding for a considerable proportion of the work on Minimum Income Standards which is very welcome,' Sr Bernadette continues. 'Without it we could not have continued to employ our two research associates on a contract basis.' This work provides policy and decision makers with facts and figures on the expenditure and income which households require to have a minimum acceptable standard of living. 'There is a growing realisation at EU level that minimum income standards are a valuable tool in the eradication of poverty,' she adds.

Sister Bernadette also points out how the Daughters of Charity made available temporary accommodation at their North William Street premises. With Department of the Environment support, this facility was converted into twenty self-contained apartments, the Rendu apartments, named after Sr Rosalie Rendu, a Daughter of Charity closely associated with Fréderic Ozanam and the foundation of the SVP in Paris in 1833. Offering short-term accommodation to homeless people with special needs, the Rendu apartments were opened by the Minister for the Environment, Brendan Howlin, TD, in October 1995 and are now part of DePaul[3].

---

2. February 2014.

3. Formerly the De Paul Trust, DePaul was founded by the Society of St Vincent de Paul in the Republic of Ireland in 2002 and in Northern Ireland in 2005. It is now a separate cross-border charity helping people most in need with a particular mission to end homelessness and change the lives of those affected by it.

SVP involvement in the Vincentian Partnership is strong. Larry Tuomey is its current chairperson. In the early stages, Noel was an inspirational, encouraging speaker at partnership gatherings. 'He was very much in favour of the partnership. I had great admiration for him. He had lovely personable qualities. We were all devastated when he died and, of course, felt very much for Anne and the family,' remarks Sr Bernadette quietly. She points to a collection of photographs on top of a bookshelf in the Partnership Office. She picks up one of Noel's memoriam cards, looks at the picture and says, 'He's a great loss'.

## Common cause

As suggested, Noel's inclination to co-operate, to be a team player, to emphasise what people had in common rather than what divided them, was strong. He preferred to avoid conflict and division. He was good at mediating, an honest broker with a facility for finding common ground. If there was a possibility that an issue would be better addressed jointly, then Noel leaned towards collaboration. Larry Tuomey believes that Noel's involvement with the Vincentian Partnership brought renewed vigour to the society. Similarly, Noel was instrumental in the De Paul Trust coming to Dublin and sat on their board until his death in 2003.

## Children's rights

Anne Murphy, a former SVP Youth Officer, cites a typical example of Noel's co-operative disposition. In the early days of the twenty-first century, CSPE (Civic, Social and Political Education) was still a relatively fragile new subject in schools. SVP joined with the Children's Rights Alliance, the Combat Poverty Agency and the Equality Authority in developing a website for the subject. The result was a powerful resource that enabled learners to explore themes related to the rights of children. Incidentally, on the website, one of the key quotes for classroom discussion was from Noel Clear: 'Poverty and inequality exist because those with power can structure society in their own interests'.

## Working together locally

Given Noel was national president, there is a strong emphasis here on leadership within the SVP. However, as a ten thousand-strong organisation in Ireland, grassroots members provide its lifeblood. Noel worked hard at remaining close to members. Two anonymous SVP members volunteered short accounts of how they got involved and how they see their roles. Their perspectives illustrate some of the motivations that also drove Noel.

'I suppose I'm a typical enough member of the SVP in that it was always something at the back of my mind that I often said I should do, though I didn't join my local conference until I was in my fifties,' says Andrew[4]. 'That was eight years ago. Having said that, I think it's important to point out that we are a more diverse bunch than you might imagine,' he adds.

'I've worked in a variety of jobs,' he continues, 'but when I was behind the bar I saw a lot of people the worse for wear. When you work in a pub you ask yourself – who looks after these people? Then I would have been aware from the telly of the work that various charities do. I remember a conversation with a young guy who went off to spend a year working in an asylum in the Lebanon. I thought to myself, surely that is real Christianity. Why doesn't everyone do something like this, I asked myself. Why don't I do something more? At that stage of my life I suppose I felt I wanted to give back something to society so I joined,' he says.

Through his local conference and SVP area meetings, Andrew has observed a wide cross section of members. He says:

I suspect a lot of people share that idea of wanting to make

---

4. Pseudonym.

a contribution, to be Christian in a practical way. With the younger ones it might be that they are people who might have been drawn to religious orders in the past but find the V de P[5] more attractive. Although, as I said, we are a diverse bunch. Some members would feel quite alienated from the Church after the sex abuse scandals and cover ups but still have this commitment to helping poorer people. When you look at the other scandals associated with so many charities, many are angry about that too. The V de P is attractive because the money goes to those in need, it's less diluted.

I think when you get involved in a V de P conference, your eyes are opened to a lot of suffering. Many people struggle to get by. Everything is relative; there might not be that many out there who are starving but many parents are stressed by so many demands – costs associated with schools, clothing for their children, the price of food, every family needs a car and so on. I've seen how much they deprive themselves for the sake of their kids. We also see the devastation caused by addictions – gambling, alcohol and other drugs. It is shocking. I was surprised how often social workers refer people to the V de P. Indeed, in general, I'm not impressed by the way various local authorities fail to meet people's needs. Joining the V de P has definitely made me more aware of the limitations of so many services. I'm much more critical of them now. And in the conference we never have enough money to meet the needs of so many people utterly deserving of support.

Of course, the V de P is not a perfect organisation. At times, I think it's a mirror of Irish society, diverse, at times proprietorial, competitive, even petty. Some conferences are

---

5. While SVP has been used widely throughout the book as shorthand for Society of St Vincent de Paul, 'V de P' is also commonly used and was the term preferred by Andrew, and was also subsequently used by Clodagh in the next section, hence its use here.

very focused on their own local area and don't necessarily see the bigger picture. In one area you could have a conference getting maybe ten times the donations of another. The richer ones should pass the money up the line.

It would be good if the average age of members in our conference was lower. We could do with some younger blood but I can see how demanding even a few hours a week might be for someone up to their eyes with small children... No, I have no regrets about joining the SVP.

### A privilege

'The conference I joined two years ago is very fortunate in that we range in age from the twenties to the seventies,' says Clodagh.[6] 'The conference works in a part of Dublin where there are increased requests for financial help from people who cannot make ends meet,' she explains. 'We are meeting more and more new homeless families and people who cannot make ends meet often through no fault of their own – people losing jobs, getting into debt, living hand to mouth. Even though I work as a pharmacist, my SVP experience had been both an eye-opener and a privilege. Being able to support people in need, offering some practical help, listening and letting people be heard is part of the privilege. It makes you appreciate your own life more, gives you new perspectives and helps you not to sweat the small stuff too much,' Clodagh adds.

'I suspect that like lots of people I had always considered the idea of "giving something back" over the years but never quite got around to it,' she continues. 'Yes, I am fortunate that I come from a caring family where reaching out to others is valued. Like many other young professionals I was busy forging my career but, of course, at the back of my mind were those big question

---

6. Pseudonym.

like "What's it all about?" A lightbulb moment occurred at Mass one Sunday. The president of the SVP conference spoke, inviting people to give a few hours each week visiting people seeking help. He talked about it as a privilege. I then met him for a chat. He emphasised that what was needed was a sympathetic ear, a firm handshake and to be a good listener. I became part of the team visiting families on a weekly basis. I got to see the practical value of assistance through food vouchers and paying bills, offering financial help, guiding people to MABS[7] and so on. I remember one man who had been without a home who was allocated a flat but there was no cooker. V de P organised the delivery of a cooker. Shortly before Christmas we got a card which stated: "thanks so much to SVP for all the help before Christmas with the cooker. For the first time in my life I feel like I have a home. Happy Christmas". We had made a small difference', she remarks.

Clodagh and her volunteer colleagues get on well and they often visit the pub after a meeting and make a point of going out for a meal together a few times during the year. 'I think there are lots of people of my generation who want to give something back to society. We're also a generation willing to try out new things. In an organisation like the SVP, with a long tradition and maybe some old-fashioned practices, I think it's important to see the bigger picture, the many layers of poverty, the need for creative responses and a willingness to accommodate members from diverse backgrounds. In our conference we focus on shared goals rather than on age differences. When you listen to people's hardships and struggles in life you become more aware of how great their needs are,' she says. 'Personally, with lower Mass attendances than in the past, I'd like to see the SVP coming up with new ways of recruiting young volunteers,' she concludes.

---

7. Money Advice and Budgeting Service.

# Chapter 25
## The Practical Christian

While Noel may have embodied the qualities of a practical Christian, when it came to fixing things around the house, it was a different story. 'DIY wasn't his thing,' says Anne politely, adding, 'but he was keen on trying to do things.' She illustrates this with a story. 'There was a little wooden shed in the garden, nearly falling down. Noel decided he was going to do a little job to secure the roof. Without checking, he went up onto the roof and it gave way. Next thing his legs were dangling through it. He wasn't hurt. Instead of going to help, I ran in and got a camera to photograph the event. We had many a laugh over that.'

Conor thinks that a lot of the funny stories about Noel are because, as he puts it: 'his brain was always on, often to do with the SVP. His absent-mindedness was because he was focussed on matters Vincentian.' However, he wasn't totally impractical. Once, while on holidays in Wales, a very young Conor was in the front of the car and released the handbrake. As he remembers: 'it was like something from an action movie, Mam and Dad running after the car as it headed for a reservoir.' Anne adds, 'It hit a stone and slowed enough to allow Noel time to jump into the car and rescue Conor and bring the car to a halt. I still have nightmares about that,' she says.

## Inspiring leader

Audry Deane worked for more than a decade as an SVP social policy officer. She recalls Noel's gentle manner, his ability to listen and his inspiring leadership. Noel's awareness that Christianity is never only about feeding the hungry or nursing the wounded but must also ask questions about the causes of such conditions, impressed her. With specific responsibilities for health and education, Audry saw how Noel's vision of the SVP as a credible critic of government policies developed. She speaks quite positively about her experiences with government departments. 'With Health, and Social Protection and more recently Children and Youth Affairs, I do think they are genuinely interested in hearing the SVP point of view.'

Initially, Audry's experience with the Department of Education was disappointing. 'It's amazing how different the culture is from one department to the next,' she says. 'Education has been very inward-looking, not very proactive and, of course, there are a lot of strong vested interests,' she remarks. Our conversation took place when ASTI opposition to Junior Cycle reform was particularly strident and strong lobby groups' attachment to the status quo seemed the norm. High-profile rows like that also heighten the impression that it's a 'Department for Schools' rather than sufficiently concerned with wider educational issues. Audry tempers her remarks with an account of how, in 2012, SVP gathered signatures calling on the department to be more proactive about school book rental schemes. 'It was great to be able to present those ten thousand names directly to Minister Ruiarì Quinn. In fairness to him, I think he took this seriously.'

Relative success on the book rental front encouraged Audry and her colleagues. 'We teamed up with Barnardos and highlighted how ridiculously expensive some uniforms are.' Again, their case was listened to; now schools are obliged to consult parents about any uniform changes. Audry sees this as one practical outcome of the work of analysis, advocacy and campaigning. 'I'd like to think Noel is smiling at these achievements,' she adds.

Audrey adds that 'because of his very personable manner, I think people often underestimated Noel. He didn't raise his voice. He didn't thump the table. So, some thought he was a pushover. But he was incredibly dogged and very strategic. He knew what he wanted to achieve. He always had an eye for the bigger picture. When you were with him, he was always very present to you. When Nelson Mandela died and there was an avalanche of comment, I remember thinking of Noel. In his own way, Noel too was a world citizen: the gentle manner, the smile for everyone, the big vision, the determination to fight poverty, the doggedness and smart way of working. Noel had depth and genuineness. He was humble. He had great empathy with people. You knew there was great inner strength. I think he had a deep understanding of suffering'.

## Strengths and weaknesses

Tom McSweeney, a national vice-president of the SVP, has a unique overview of the society's strengths and vulnerabilities. 'Volunteers on the ground at local conference level have a keen awareness of people's needs, of how poverty impacts on individual people and families. Over one hundred and fifty years, SVP had earned the trust of the public and the society is regarded as a credible voice for social justice,' he says. But Tom knows that past achievements don't necessarily guarantee future success. 'Irish society has been undergoing great change. Attracting fresh volunteers is a challenge as people's lives have become so busy. Also, as we explore this difficult concept of 'social justice' we can see that the SVP is not simply about "the poor", it has to involve discussion about ethics, about what kind of Ireland we should aspire to, about a society with equality of opportunity.'

With his strong media background, Tom is acutely aware of the possibilities offered by new digital media, social networking and information technology generally. As he puts it: 'The challenge is how best to harness them to advance the work of the SVP?'

## Volunteering

Beyond the SVP, Noel saw volunteering as vital to any society and was not shy about asserting this. He regularly called on leaders of both Church and state to highlight the tradition and ethos of voluntary service. He knew some organisations were finding it difficult to recruit new volunteers. Lifestyle changes, including time spent working and commuting, has rendered volunteering more challenging.

The Keogh Square experiences had taught Noel how powerful the energy and enthusiasm of young adults can be. While respecting the tradition of typical SVP members being older, he actively sought new young recruits. Noel also knew that many people, obliged to retire from paid work at age sixty-five, still had much to contribute to society. He pondered how voluntary groups might harness this expertise and goodwill without alienating younger volunteers?[1]

The government published *A White Paper on Supporting Voluntary Activity, Developing the Relationship between the State and the Community and Voluntary Sector* in 2000 and set up a national committee on volunteering. Chaired by Chris Flood TD, the group reported in 2002. Noel, as SVP President, was an active member of the committee. The report sets out possibilities and obstacles associated with volunteering. It recognises that voluntary activity

---

1. See, for example, *The Irish Times*, 8 December 1999 which reported on an SVP press conference where Noel as National President, Larry Tuomey, Dublin Regional President and Columba Faulkner, National Secretary, mapped out some of the challenges and opportunities for volunteering arising from lifestyle changes.

is central to community development; encouraging volunteering should be a key social goal, enabled by government policies.

Put briefly, voluntary activity builds and sustains a society. Volunteering can be seen as one expression of our civic selves, a type of public assertion that we are connected with other people in a community, usually for the common good. Whatever our motives – belief in a cause or an idea, a need to help, to meet others or a mixture of these – we find ourselves relating to others who think or act similarly. This in turn advances social cohesion. Indeed, many acknowledge that voluntary action for the common good is a powerful argument in favour of societal support for religious belief and practice. Volunteering is important for individuals, for organisations and for the wider society.[2]

As a volunteer himself, unpaid in any of the roles he played, Noel knew that volunteering is one of SVP's great strengths, adding credibility when lobbying policy makers and officials. While juggling his day-job with his voluntary work wasn't easy, he remained convinced of the importance of volunteering.

Nowadays, volunteering can involve Garda vetting and other checks that delay active engagement. One would hope that legitimate concerns with safeguarding children and health and safety issues would not become so restrictive that would-be volunteers – with the SVP or other groups – are deterred. How many future Noel Clears, ordinary and extraordinary young men and women, ready and willing to contribute to a youth club, conference or other group, back off because regulations seem over-complicated?

---

2. A more detailed account of the value of volunteering can be found in a paper by Freda Donoghue of the Centre for Nonprofit Management, Trinity College, Dublin at *https://ssrn.com/abstract=952672*

**Solidarity**

Derry O'Connor, the Crumlin-based youth worker mentioned earlier, later became assistant director of the City of Dublin Youth Service Board (formerly Comhairle le Leas Óige). Derry remembers Noel's strong sense of solidarity with youth workers. 'He was very aware of our work and working conditions. Pay scales in the probation and welfare service were linked to the rates paid to engineers in the public service. As youth workers, our rates were linked to that of probation officers. Whenever there was a change in pay, invariably Noel would pick up the phone and let me know because at that time you had to process your claim. Fairness was always present in his thinking.'

Overall, Derry reflecting on his contact with Noel over a thirty-year period, sums him up as 'a wonderful professional, a human being who made an immense contribution to social inclusion in Ireland, helped shape my thinking and actions and ultimately influenced the direction of youth work in Dublin city.'

# Chapter 26
## Challenging the Nation

Noel's ability to frame a crucial question and pursue it was one of his great strengths. When he was President of the Dublin Region of the SVP, he became aware that some members questioned the effectiveness of the work. There were families that SVP members had visited for generations; did this encourage dependency? Was SVP intervention making any difference in these people's lives? Noel didn't shy away from such questions.

Practical and imaginative, Noel sought and obtained support from the then Department of Social Welfare for a facilitator to work with a number of conferences. The focus was on questioning how they were working with poor families and what changes could be made. The project had limited success. More than a decade later, with Noel's persistence, the SVP National Council embarked on a strategic plan and the *Making a Difference* project adopted that same reflective thinking among conferences.

Audry Deane notes that government departments sometimes use the SVP as a sounding board for new proposals and John Monaghan talks about the society's counterparts in the UK, marvelling at the Irish organisation's access to power. 'When they hear that we had a face-to-face meeting with a government minister, or that we made a presentation to an Oireachtas committee, or were discussing specific issues with senior officials, they shake their heads in wonder,' he says.

John has been on many such delegations. Politicians, he notes, have a keen awareness of the SVP embedded in local communities, operating in every parish in the country. 'You could say we are a bit like the GAA at prayer,' he jokes. 'So, even if they don't like what we say, they don't often voice that. Sometimes politicians can be a little patronising, gushing about the wonderful work the SVP does. I would prefer if they would focus more on the problems facing the people we meet every week.'

### Standing up for the voiceless

Noel's public statements during 1998 exemplify his efforts to position the SVP as a prophetic, challenging voice. Two main themes emerge. The first is based on SVP members' experiences and focuses on the 'damage and degradation visited on too many people in Ireland through their marginalisation and exclusion from the benefits of the newly-resurgent economy.' Noel saw the rising economic tide as a unique moment for the state to cherish the children of the nation equally. The second strand was how he challenged SVP members to be faithful to applying Ozanam's principles to local situations.

### Budget commentary

SVP's robust responses to the budget for 1999 further illustrate Noel's challenging voice. He was happy to align the society with a range of other commentators with like-minded perspectives. For example, Noel supported the comments from Noreen Byrne of the National Women's Council that children had lost out in the budget and that the cabinet 'has chosen to ignore that there is a major crisis in child-care'. He agreed with Hugh Frazer of the

Combat Poverty Agency that the budget would make little impact on the high cost of rearing children. Noel himself, on behalf of the SVP, acknowledged the commitment in the budget to tax reform for the lower paid but said that the welfare increases proposed fell far short of what was required and that child benefit rises were derisory. He also asserted that 'the long-term unemployed in particular are feeling more and more marginalised than ever before in the Celtic Tiger when they see the spending power of the public at large and powerful advertising campaigns'.

The SVP critique of the budget generated an editorial in the *Evening Herald* headed 'Poverty must be a political issue', noting the SVP observation that 'despite the Celtic Tiger and a £1.4bn budget surplus, two hundred thousand Irish people are now dependent on the society to survive'.

As well as using such occasions to generate funds for SVP work, Noel frequently inserted bigger questions. What kind of society are we creating? What models do we need to really care for the less well off? How can we reinforce a sense of community throughout Ireland which is threatened by new pressures and life-patterns? How can we all exercise our social responsibilities? How can politicians best serve the community?[1]

Patsy McGarry in *The Irish Times* captured Noel's questioning well, in December 1998, when he reported him framing the challenge thus: 'We need to ask the question as to whether the competitive nature of society and the burning desire for wealth and material goods tends to crush compassion and respect for those on the margins.' That report is accompanied by a powerful front-page photograph of Noel.

---

1. These questions are based on a report in the *Catholic Standard*, 11 December 1998.

## Robust positioning

As the economic boom rolled on Noel became more vocal about the less comfortable features of 'improvements'. He felt that as society 'progressed', the marginalised were becoming more isolated and forgotten. For example, the *Irish Examiner* reported on 13 October 2001 on the SVP's sharp-edged pre-budget submission. The headline reads: 'Boom Times Ignores Plight of 1m Irish, says charity'. Chief political correspondent John Dowling wrote, 'Ireland is the most business-friendly country in the developed world – but just about the worst place to live if you are poor, the St Vincent de Paul Society said last night'. The report continued:

> In an extremely hard-hitting pre-budget submission, the country's most popular domestic charity challenged Finance Minister Charlie McCreevy to take radical action on behalf of one million Irish people excluded from the country's new-found prosperity. SVP President Noel Clear said the contrast between the key economic and social indicators vividly showed what an unfair place Ireland had become.

The newspaper report shows how well Noel and his colleagues had done their homework backing up their assertions with facts and figures. They spelled out specific demands to the Minister for Finance, especially in relation to welfare, education, health, housing, childcare and child benefit. Noel and the social justice team believed budgets were occasions 'to deal a major blow to poverty and inequality'. That *Irish Examiner* report concluded, 'No one has the right to consign vulnerable and less economically productive citizens to a second-class life,' Mr Clear said.

Ministers for Finance are subject to a great barrage of interests and it would be naïve to overestimate the effects of any one pre-budget submission. However, the quality of SVP submissions adds to the society's standing both in the court of public opinion and with politicians and policy makers. Of course, that never made Noel and his work immune from criticism.

An *Examiner* headline in late 1998 read, 'Sex abusers and rapists in Curragh Jail benefit from society's charity'[2]. Responding, Noel stated that the SVP abhorred all crimes against the person, particularly those of a sexual or abusive nature. However, everyone was entitled to charity, especially at Christmas. He added that SVP conferences regularly befriend those in prison, noting that, isolated from their families, prisoners find Christmas tough. He said that the SVP 'reaches out to everybody in need and people who are in prison, no matter what their offences, are in need'.

### Ensuring that nobody is marginalised

In 2000, Noel was invited to address the congregation during the annual Novena at the shrine to Our Lady at Knock, Co. Mayo on 15 August. He began by referring to the challenges in the recent bishops' pastoral letter, *Prosperity with a Purpose: Christian Faith and Values in a Time of Rapid Economic Growth.* While welcoming recent economic progress, especially the decrease in the number of unemployed people, Noel noted that 'we still have poverty in the midst of all this success,' quoting the bishops: 'The first duty of the citizen towards the common good is to ensure that nobody is marginalised and to bring back into the community those who have been marginalised in the past.' Noel touched on many familiar themes: Ozanam; Paris 1833; poverty; justice; Ireland 2000; Gospel values; cherishing all the children of the nation equally; a caring society; family; the voiceless; the marginalised; SVP conference members' weekly visitations; homelessness; prisoners; psychiatric patients; the new often hidden poor; refugees.

---

2. 31 December 1998.

Noel acknowledged how scandals had rocked so many institutions, including the alarming extent of child sex abuse, abuse of power in the political arena and low standards in the business and commercial sectors. He juxtaposed greed with justice, care and compassion for all citizens, referencing the recent SVP *Social Policy Manifesto* which saw common values of equality, solidarity, self-sufficiency and participation as underpinning 'the work of our organisation'. Noel linked these ideas with the day's liturgy, in particular 'Yahweh asks of you only this: to act justly, to love tenderly and to walk humbly with your God'(Micah 6:8) and 'If one of your brothers or one of the sisters is in need of clothes and has not enough food to live on and one of you says to them – I wish you well, keep yourself warm and eat plenty – without giving them the bare necessities of life, then what good is that?'(James, 2:15).

Noel said such perspectives constituted 'a huge challenge to the Christian Church, and indeed, particularly now for the laity.' Noel concluded by focussing on justice, respect, compassion and forgiveness, quoting Ozanam, 'we must make love accomplish what justice and law alone can never do'.

# Chapter 27
## Criticisms and Beyond

Noel's efforts to bring a more professional edge to the organisation, to develop a culture where volunteers and paid employees worked in constructive and complementary ways, were not universally appreciated. Decisions to employ additional staff brought criticisms from members who emphasised the SVP's voluntary character. In some regions this was quite pronounced. Noel didn't enjoy the criticisms but was convinced that to advocate effectively on behalf of marginalised people at a national level, the SVP needed to recruit specialists. He often put it like this: 'We needed people who could do the analysis, make the case, and, very practically, be available during the daytime.'

While careful never to align the SVP with any political party or ideology, Noel often had to field irate phone calls, letters and personal encounters from members who were uncomfortable with what they saw as the SVP becoming 'too political.'[1]

---

1. Given Noel's social justice concerns, the reader may reasonably wonder about his party political inclinations. As an eighteen year old it appears that Noel did attend a Fianna Fáil Ard Fheis but subsequently was careful not to align himself with any particular party, happy to approach politicians of all parties seeking support for the work of the SVP.

## Too bland?

Less frequently, criticisms that the SVP was too bland, not sharp enough in critiquing policies that perpetuate poverty, surfaced. Noel also took these seriously. In December 1997, Fr Jackie Robinson, a parish priest in Co. Laois[2], criticised the 'gentle, mild-mannered people' in the SVP for using 'lovely mellow language' meekly chiding the government; he wished to see a more vociferous edge to the SVP, akin to farmers' lobby groups and trade unions. Noel welcomed this kind of criticism as it encouraged him to press ahead with strengthening the social policy analysis dimension of the society's work.

Following the Robinson letter, Noel's next 'Opinion' in the SVP Bulletin[3] opened with a declaration that SVP founder Fréderic Ozanam 'got it right' when he said: 'It is a matter of grave social concern whether society is to be merely a means of exploitation for the benefit of the strong, or the dedication of each for the benefit of all – especially the weak'. He developed this theme, citing sobering statistics including two hundred and seventeen thousand unemployed, the highest level of functional illiteracy in the OECD and the growing number of people begging on the streets. Noel then addressed the growth of a culture of individual competitiveness, the rise of the 'intensely competitive and increasingly vulnerable ethos of contract-working,' the growing gap between the richest and the poorest and the soaring prices of houses and apartments. He noted how 1998 figures for record car sales, house prices, a booming restaurant and leisure industry and the millions spent on music, fashion, drink, drugs and gambling are visible indicators of what many regard as 'success'. The rush for riches, legally or illegally, he observed, 'brings its own consequences'. Here he mentioned 'permanent

---

2. *The Irish Times*, 16 December 1997.
3. SVP Bulletin, 25.1. Spring 1998, p. 2.

personal stress, less time for others, growing family pressures, an alcohol and drug abuse epidemic, a rising suicide rate and the fragmentation of society'. Noel observed how the marginalised, 'completely excluded from enjoying even the smallest benefit of our booming economy' often struggle just to cope with day-to-day living. He invited readers to 'look at some of the sprawling urban local authority flat and housing schemes – with dilapidated houses, graffiti-covered walls and littered streets – and you get some idea of the quality of life endured by the many families there. Consider too the quiet desperation and loneliness of those living in poverty in so many rural areas.' Hardly, bland! As we now know, the consequences of not listening to voices like Noel's, turned out to be even more disastrous.

Noel's warm, even chirpy, manner didn't change during the years of his presidency but criticisms cut deep and he did feel the weight of the office. Few other people in the country in voluntary, unpaid positions, carried such onerous responsibilities.

### Inspiration

Amid the slings and arrows of criticism, Noel's family, friends and his religious beliefs sustained him. He would have been pleased to hear Archbishop Diarmuid Martin, in 2008, addressing SVP volunteers:

> The Church community must be one where no one should be left poor, that is deprived of what is needed for a dignified life. Poverty is not simply a lack of financial or material resources. Poverty is the inability of people to realise their God-given potential. Fighting poverty is about enhancing people to realise their God-given potential.

He continued:

A Church which wishes to remain true to the 'communion', the common living which was characteristic of the early Church must be one where its members and its structures work together to ensure that the caring, healing and restoring power which Jesus demonstrated in his life and teaching is made visible today, through individual lives and through forms of community witness[4].

For those who knew him, Noel was an exemplar of such witness.

'He had a great ability to relate to people,' remembers John O'Flaherty who volunteered with Noel in St Vincent's Youth Club. 'People knew they could trust him. He did what he said. He would never make a promise he couldn't keep. I was always astonished at his ability to retain precise details about individual people. It seemed to come so naturally to him but, of course, it was driven by his deep interest in people, especially the vulnerable.'

Noel's brother, Tony, echoes these sentiments when he says, 'In later years I'd often meet Noel for lunch. I knew he was probably squeezing it in between two other meetings because he was intensely busy. But when you were with him he was totally present to you. That ability to focus on the person he was talking to was very striking,' says Tony.

Noel's attitude to people was rarely judgmental. He accepted people as they were. His wife Anne recalls how often, in conversations where people were criticised for their actions, Noel would state: 'there's good in the worst of us and bad in the best of us.'

4. *Tougher Times – Tender Hearts*, homily by Diarmuid Martin, Archbishop of Dublin and Primate of Ireland, St Vincent de Paul Dublin Regional Conference, Croke Park, 8 November 2008.

This positive disposition was also evident in Noel's attitude to SVP volunteers. While his own inspiration was rooted in his religious beliefs, he never questioned others' motivations. Some SVP personnel voice a concern that the society has been moving away from its Vincentian roots. Noel was keen to respect the diversity of perspectives among SVP staff and volunteers. Credibility, he believed, derived primarily from actions. SVP volunteers and staff are attracted by the actual work. The extent to which they share a commitment to friendship, support, solidarity, justice and help towards self-sufficiency can vary. Similarly, inspiration from the lives of Fréderic Ozanam, Vincent de Paul, Louise de Marillac or Jesus Christ also differs. One senior figure acknowledges that people whose faith in mainstream Church activities has been weakened because of abuse and cover-up scandals remain willing to associate themselves with the SVP.

## Looking forward

Conscious of his formative experiences, Noel was enthusiastic about projects that heightened young people's awareness of poverty and other social issues. Ever since leading the Council of Youth Clubs, he was always willing to attend SVP youth gatherings such as rallies in Kerdiffstown House, Co Kildare or leaders' get-togethers in Carne, Co. Wexford.

As Dublin regional president, Noel initiated Youth gatherings in Kerdiffstown that were characterised by lively debate and discussion. An account of the second Dublin Regional Youth Rally in 1991 notes that speakers included Paul Cummins, Rose McGowan, Bill Cleary, Noel himself, Fr Peter McVerry SJ, District Justice Gillian Hussey and TDs Emmet Stagg, Eric Byrne and Mary Flaherty. Joe Duffy of RTÉ chaired a question and answer session. That report also states that during the night Noel claimed to have heard the voice of Kerdiffstown House's legendary ghost – 'Tom's Victim'!

As national president, Noel initiated positions of SVP youth development officers, one of whom, Anne Murphy, brought experience, insight and energy to the role between 1998 and 2006. Anne was member of an SVP conference in Monkstown Co. Dublin. This group, in collaboration with Dún Laoghaire Rathdown County Council, had set up a resource centre. As well as engaging in family visitation, members formed a homework club for children in the area. 'We needed volunteers to assist us in that work,' recalls Anne, 'so I approached schools and we enlisted some great teachers,' she says. 'When I saw the ad for the youth development officer, I thought it was a perfect position for me,' she recalls.

Anne's job was to support schools, youth groups and students in higher education to develop greater poverty awareness, prompt them to analyse the issues and take suitable action. In secondary schools, she directed her support mainly at teachers of subjects such as religious education and CSPE (Civic, Social and Political Education). Transition year students were also a key target group. While fundraising within schools is important, it is far from the only interest of the SVP, Anne remarked. She revamped the SVP education pack, building it around ten well-thought-out lessons, with worksheets and ideas for action projects. The origins of the SVP, the meaning of poverty and social exclusion, financial poverty, homelessness, Travellers, refugees and asylum seekers were among the issues addressed in the pack. The SVP Justice for Youth Action project enabled young people to research a topic, take appropriate action and then exhibit their work. For Anne, a highlight was a showcase event for two hundred and fifty transition year students from around the country in the National Basketball Arena in Tallaght.

Anne warmly recalls Noel's support. 'He was inspirational. Noel was such a compassionate man. He believed in listening to young people. When he spoke he was able to give them a true sense of what is involved in giving of oneself to others less fortunate. Noel recognised that young people are the future of the SVP and they need to be nurtured and supported,' remembers Anne.

Anne also brought the SVP message to other youth groups including third level students. She frequently reminded her audiences that Fréderic Ozanam was a student when he and his colleagues founded the SVP in Paris in 1833. Their initiative continues to inspire and to exemplify youthful dynamism and impatience in the face of injustice leading to action. Today, some of the most vibrant SVP conferences in Ireland are in higher education colleges.

'I loved the way young people enthusiastically deal with a problem that others may have given up on long ago. They bring new insights, skills and energy. I loved the way they challenged the society to remember that young people's needs are different. I could see how engagement with SVP added fresh meaning to being Christian, how it nurtured a living committed faith and spirituality,' comments Anne.

### Fundraising

Noel was sensitive to SVP's history and its position as one of the country's largest and most credible charitable organisations. He knew, in detail, the centrality of fundraising in the SVP and that many families and individuals depended on weekly support. But Noel never avoided difficult questions around fundraising. He never liked charities competing with each other. He was conflicted about employing advertising and public relations agencies. He often asked whether charity work temporarily shores up problems that require long-term structured, state interventions. He also knew that charity can demean human dignity. Ever practical, he often commented that getting a job could radically transform a person's life in a way charity handouts never could.

During Noel's time as SVP president, a political discussion centred on whether Ireland was spiritually closer to Boston or Berlin, a shorthand way of contrasting low taxation regimes with those offering high levels of public services. In the United States, there is a strong tradition of charity, or philanthropy. 80 per cent of Americans give, on average, two per cent of their overall incomes, to non-profit organisations. But despite such impressive, private generosity in a wealthy country, the US has higher poverty rates than most other 'developed' countries, and millions of Americans lack access to health care and safe, affordable housing. This US charity tradition prompts questions about giving as 'a moral safety valve'; does donating to charities keep us from confronting underlying injustices in society? As one commentator[5] remarks: 'Charity may not be very effective at alleviating long-term poverty, but it is quite good at relieving our sense of guilt about it'. While Noel knew that rich-poor divisions in Ireland are less pronounced than in the USA, this issue was a constant concern.

## Reimagining SVP conferences

Noel's questioning of traditions also led him, in 2002, to initiate a conference development project. The goal was straightforward enough: improving both how conferences worked in responding to people experiencing poverty and exclusion, and how they worked within themselves. Judith King of Community Action Network (CAN) was engaged to facilitate the project. 'This initiative was important,' explains Liam O'Dwyer, 'because it was addressing the need for responses by the SVP to individuals and their circumstances to be complemented by a community development

---

5. F. Quigley, 'The Limits of Philanthropy', *Commonweal*, 8 January 2015.

approach.' Liam adds that this project was an excellent illustration of how well Noel and Larry Tuomey, then president of the Dublin Region, worked together and with another agency. To give the work focus, Noel posed some questions. Are 'handouts' or 'brown envelopes' the most effective way of supporting people? Does our work promote dependency? What does 'befriending' actually mean in practice? Who are most in need in today's Ireland? How might we best recruit new volunteers? As well as focusing on targets, goals and outcomes, can we look at the processes we use at meetings and gatherings?

This was a brave undertaking, almost inevitably guaranteed to arouse criticisms. Liam O'Dwyer remarks, 'I thought he was courageous in asking conferences to look at themselves, to pose questions about handouts, to justify their actions. I always liked the way Noel could operate at the intellectual, visionary and practical levels.'

**Back to school**

Noel was especially pleased when he was contacted by Kieran McGinley, president of the Past Pupils Union of Westland Row CBS, his former school. There was a tradition of selecting an annual 'RowMan of the Year' and Noel was the man for 2000. Previous recipients included soccer players Jackie Carey, Gerry Mackey and Ray Tracey, actor Cyril Cusack, hotelier PV Doyle, musician Shay Healy and world champion snooker player Ken Doherty. Anne and Conor, Alan and Rory as well as twin brother Seán accompanied Noel to the event on 7 January and he was delighted to accept the award. Noel recalled how those foundational school years had shaped his subsequent career and voluntary work.

# Chapter 28
## The Wider World

Noel saw himself as 'a homebird'; when abroad, food was especially challenging. However, SVP leadership brought with it obligations to represent Ireland in various situations, for example, in London, Glasgow, Bradford and Northampton. In 1999, along with Columba Faulkner, Mary Toole, Gabriel Fay, Gerry Martin and others, Noel and Anne travelled to Fatima in Portugal for an SVP World Plenary.

In 2001, the worldwide SVP formed an International Executive Committee, a group of leaders from five continents to co-ordinate policies and activities. Noel represented Ireland at the first meeting in Almeida, Spain. Noel said, 'I always had a strong feeling of solidarity at these gatherings. The realisation that so many people are joined by a common thread of care and compassion for the marginalised through our many works of service is very powerful.' The topics were engaging: communication, finance, young people, members' training and spiritual formation and a new initiative VinPaz – Vincentians for Peace. The latter aimed to respond to special needs globally with the participation of full-time volunteers.

In this international arena, Noel discovered a close ally in Jim O'Connor, representing the SVP in England and Wales. 'We had many conversations about the development of the society in these islands,' remembers Jim. 'Noel would introduce the discussion with the question: are we winning? He was deeply concerned about making the society more fit-for-purpose in its vocation to serve the poor,' he says. 'I know Noel was courageous in his attempts to bring change to the SVP in Ireland, particularly in equipping members to address poverty effectively in the modern age'. Jim adds, 'Noel was a good man in every sense, as regards his family, his faith, the Society and its objectives. He was a man of humour. He had a leaning towards the arts, especially music and I don't mean his unique take on Dickie Rock! Noel was a consummate Irishman and he never failed to begin an address to any meeting in his native tongue.'

Like almost everyone else who rubbed shoulders with Noel when abroad, Jim O'Connor remembers his slightly bizarre take on food. 'You could say his dietary requirements became a matter of international concern,' says Jim, smiling. 'He seemed to be only at ease with carbohydrates. One occasion, in Rome, at an international meeting, remains in the memory. Noel arrived late in the evening at the hotel and discovered that there were no chips or anything similar on the menu. A group of American Vincentians, fearful that he might starve to death, took it upon themselves to drive him around the Eternal City in search of the aforementioned chips. They did eventually find them,' laughs Jim.

Subsequently Noel's international role expanded when he took on the position of co-ordinator with the General Council of the SVP for Ireland, Scotland, England and Wales.

## Following the inspiration

One of Anne's warmest memories is of a trip Noel, herself and other Vincentians made in 2001, following the footsteps of Saint Vincent de Paul. They began in Paris visiting places familiar from the Ozanam beatification, particularly locations in Rue de Sèvres and Rue de Bac. A long coach journey to Dax, Vincent de Paul's birthplace in south-west France followed. 'Maybe eight hours long,' remembers Anne. 'On the way we stopped in a forest and a Vincentian priest Fr Frank Mullan said Mass at a picnic table. It was simple and very moving. No ostentation and very spiritual. Beautiful. We were surrounded by birds and other wildlife,' she recalls.

### Global concerns

Food tastes notwithstanding, Noel's international work broadened his awareness of global issues. In 2002, he located the work of local conferences in the context of the 'fight against hunger throughout the world'. 'Beginning on our own doorstep, each conference must make sure that no one in their catchment area suffers from hunger in any form,' he wrote. But, Noel continued, SVP is challenged 'to look around the world and see the many countries where people, young and old, are starving to death.' He cited the SVP twinning tradition as a practical vehicle for making 'a small contribution to alleviating the suffering of the African people'.

Surveys consistently show SVP, Concern and Trócaire as among the best known and the most strongly supported charities in Ireland. The latter two are valued and appreciated for their work with poor and marginalised people abroad, the SVP for its care for those living in poverty in Ireland. SVP twinning with conferences in Africa is less well-known.

This initiative began in 1960, initially with four conferences. Nowadays each SVP region is twinned with an African country, usually one where English is spoken widely. The East Region is twinned with Zambia, the North East with Kenya and Uganda; South West with Nigeria; Mid West with Sierra Leone; West with Malawi; North East and Midlands with Zimbabwe; South East with Gambia and Tanzania, and North with Ghana and Botswana. An impressive list!

The SVP twinning concept underlines the worldwide nature of poverty, highlights global solidarity and reminds everyone in wealthier countries of the relative nature of being poor. The main thrust of the twinning idea is with food production; Irish conferences provide support for seed, fertiliser and irrigation projects that encourage self-sufficiency. The food production focus resonates with the assistance the SVP in France gave to Ireland during the famine in the 1840s.

Asked how much money conferences should send to partner conferences, Mary Toole, a long-time champion of the twinning concept, used to cite the UN idea of so-called 'developed' countries like Ireland giving 0.7 per cent of Gross National Product (GNP) to poorer ones. Mary suggested that the SVP at local level should replicate the 0.7 per cent. In 2000, Mary calculated that in the previous decade SVP's income in Ireland was £148,400,000, £1,155,990 of which was channelled through twinning. This works out at just above the 0.7 per cent figure.

## To Southern Africa

Enthusiasm for the twinning projects, led Noel and Mary Toole to visit SVP counterparts in southern Africa in April 2002. Among those to greet them at Gabarone Airport in Botswana were John and Angela, he a Passionist priest from Mount Argus, she a Cross and Passion sister originally from Co. Tyrone. In the Kagisong Conference Centre, SVP volunteers from Zambia, Zimbabwe, Malawi, South Africa, Namibia, Lesotho, Swaziland and Botswana exchanged experiences and viewpoints with the Irish visitors.

The following day, volunteers from Sudan, Ethiopia, Kenya, Tanzania, Uganda, Malawi and Zambia conversed with Mary and Noel. Among the items discussed, Noel recalled, was how every national council might have a computer, or, if not, at least a fax machine. They also talked about training of members, education, various projects and financial accountability.

Landlocked Botswana, one of the smallest and most sparsely populated African countries – its population was then less than two million people – fascinated Noel and Mary. Three-quarters of Botswana is desert (Kalahari) though extensive diamond deposits enrich the economy. In 2002 Botswana had one of the highest incidences of AIDS per head of population. Government policy meant that orphaned children should not be institutionalised. However, grandparents often had little or no financial resources to rear the children and so homes with about ten children and a house mother, known as SOS Homes, had been established by the government and SVP was supporting these. Mary and Noel had strong memories of a visit to one of them.

Because of the uncertain political situation in Zimbabwe, the Irish Department of Foreign Affairs had advised Mary and Noel not to travel there. Hence, the Zimbabwean SVP president and administrator met them in Botswana. The Irish pair heard graphic accounts of dreadful poverty. 'There and then we promised to do more fundraising to help areas under threat of famine, like much of Zimbabwe,' recalled Mary afterwards.

Noel and Mary packed in further visits, to families, to schools, to housing projects and to other SVP volunteers before travelling to Malawi. The experience was especially memorable and both subsequently recalled vividly the magnificent green scenery, the hundreds of colourfully dressed people walking the roadsides, the looming threat of famine and the enthusiasm of the SVP members they encountered. All twenty-three SVP conferences were strapped for cash. To help the poor, some depended on 'secret bag' collections, others on small amounts given by priests. Malawi's SVP president, Patrick Namanja, hosted the Irish visitors in his village of Thyolo. They also met John McAdam who had set up the first SVP conference in Malawi in 1968. Two distinct images from Malawi haunted the visitors. One was the primary school with almost two thousand students, eight teachers and some classrooms without desks or seats. The second was the failed maize crop and what it signalled.

Former President of Ireland and UN Commissioner for Human Rights, Mary Robinson, often remarks that a persistent feature in her travels to some of the poorest people on the planet is the Irish missionary presence, often quiet and understated. The long-term solidarity of Irish priests, nuns, brothers and lay people with poor and oppressed people is a strong tradition. Perhaps unsurprisingly, the parish priest in the Ndirande township in Malawi's capital Blantyre was Fr Seamus Foley, from Ballinakill, Co. Laois. There had been an SVP conference in Ndirande for more than thirty years. In a moment of serendipity, Noel and Seamus realised they had met before, in 1962. As a young Spiritan priest, Fr Seamus had been chaplain to the Legion of Mary branch in Inchicore when Noel was a member. They quickly bridged the forty-year gap, swapping stories about SVP, Inchicore, Spiritans they both knew, the priest's time in Nigeria and Noel's role as national president. Small world indeed!

Before returning to Ireland, Noel and Mary stopped briefly in South Africa, visiting a senior citizens' home, a project for orphaned children, a hospice for terminally-ill AIDs patients, and a centre for disabled children. Back home, both worked to strengthen links with African groups and since 2002 the SVP's global dimension has expanded.

Anne says that the trip to Africa was 'very basic'. 'Noel and Mary Toole were put up by local SVP in their villages. In one case the husband moved out and Noel got his bed. Mary shared another bed with the wife. Toilets were rudimentary. I remember

Noel being struck by how simple the children's requests were: some only wanted a football. The trip to Africa was an important one for him.'

## Chapter 29
# An Untimely Departure

Noel retired from the Probation and Welfare Service in September 2001. His term as SVP President concluded on 26 May 2002. Following these two massive milestones in his life, he and Anne looked forward to travelling, spending more time together and enjoying a well-earned retirement. However, while Noel may have finished his paid employment, maintaining some voluntary, unpaid service was the most natural thing in the world. It was as if the SVP had become imprinted in his DNA.

Jim Guider had been a close friend and confidante of Noel from the early days in St Vincent's Youth Club. Jim combines a frank, practical down-to-earth view of the world with a warm and generous heart. Noel often sought Jim's advice on financial, legal and other matters. Jim was the one who had stopped the car in Dorset Street all those years ago, and phoned Anne Braine, kick-starting Noel and Anne's relationship. In the run up to retirement, Jim encouraged Noel to get himself checked out medically. 'One Dublin hospital was offering a deal, a full A to Z health check-up. Noel signed up and was delighted to get the all clear,' recalls Jim. This was hardly surprising as Noel, always slim and fit, had rarely been ill throughout his life.

Columba Faulkner has a clear recollection of the night Noel officially retired from the probation and welfare service. 'He chose to spend the evening at a party for elderly people in the inner city. Many of them would have known Noel from his days as a young Probation Officer visiting hostels around Dublin. He was there to help out, to dance, and of course, to sing the Dickie Rock classic "From the Candy Store on the Corner" among others. Noel was so unassuming,' she adds. It's also worth pointing out that his probation and welfare service colleagues did, at the end of October, throw a party to mark Noel's retirement.

## Health scare

An inkling of a health scare came on 19 November, 2002. Noel and Anne were driving to Kilkenny to visit a former colleague, Tom Ryan, when Noel's speech became slurred. They pulled into a petrol station near Naas. At first, it seemed like it might be a stroke. When Noel passed out, an ambulance was called. The diagnosis, in St James's Hospital, Dublin, revealed a tumour growing on Noel's brain. Even more shocking was the news that it was quite large and in a particularly vulnerable part of the head. Tests in St James's were followed by surgery in Beaumont Hospital. The devastating verdict was that Noel had probably twelve months to live. Initially, everyone clung to the hope that radium treatment in the Mater Hospital would be successful. But it was not to be.

Noel was home for Christmas but a growing confusion was obvious to the family. Noel persisted in trying to do normal, everyday things. Jim has vivid memories of both of them in Dillon's pub, discussing options. However, as the year unfolded, Noel's situation deteriorated. He made two special requests. One was a day trip to Cheltenham in March for the horseracing festival. Anne, Rory and Noel took a flight to Bristol, hired a car and got a prime location at the racecourse, Noel sitting on a fold-up stool. Getting close to the action was great for viewing the racing but nearly disastrous for getting home. 'We almost missed the flight, but Ryanair kept the gate open and we made it OK,' says Rory. It wasn't an easy trip for any of them, but there were no regrets.

Anne and Noel, now moving with the help of a walking stick, took a brief holiday in Jersey in July and then, in September, came Noel's second request. This time the pilgrimage was not to a racecourse but to Knock for the annual SVP gathering. Noel, Anne and Columba Faulkner took the train to Ballyhaunis where local SVP conference members brought them by car to Knock House Hotel where they stayed the night. The next day, they attended Mass in the basilica, where Noel was welcomed by name. Among the congregation was Pauline Joyce. At that stage, in September 2003, Pauline's daughter Kathryn and Rory Clear had been girlfriend and boyfriend for about six months. After Mass, Pauline introduced herself to Noel and Anne, an additional warm memory to a special outing; Rory and Kathryn married in September 2006. The journey home from Knock was difficult, requiring a wheelchair, but, again, there were no regrets.

Back in Inchicore, the family considered various options. A bed was installed downstairs and Anne, Rory, Alan and Conor became Noel's carers, quickly learning how to look after the bed-bound patient. Initially, the steroids seemed to boost his energy but, between September and December, his consciousness began to fade. As news of Noel's illness spread, family and friends visited and were always warmly welcomed.

During that difficult time, Noel's brother Seán arrived one day in Heuston Station and, facing a heavy rainstorm, hailed a taxi. As they moved through the city traffic Seán began to reminisce about the day in 1956 when Noel and himself, having received their Leaving Cert. results, took a group of boys from Keogh Square to Chipperfield's Circus. The driver listened and said, 'You know, I was one of those lads'. This stunning coincidence concluded with the driver saying: 'Say hello to Noel for me. And thanks.'

Jim Guider recalls the journey from diagnosis onwards as difficult and special. 'We had a lot of conversations. I was immensely impressed by Noel's Christian faith. He lived with the hope of recovery but knew the odds were not great. He didn't show any great fear of death. He was very brave. He took the news on the chin. He attended to the practicalities. He planned his funeral, naming who would do what, which hymns would be sung and so on. He wrote a very personal letter to the family. I don't think he had any regrets about the life he had lived. We talked about an afterlife. My faith might not have been as strong as his. He listened to my scepticism and said he still held onto what he had always believed. I could see he prayed a lot. Jesus and Mary were very big for Noel. During his life Noel didn't verbalise much about religion. I think of him as a practical Christian who lived his life well. I think he was very wary of hypocrisy. He went to Mass very regularly but was always discreet about it,' says Jim. He adds that Noel's major concern was for Anne and the boys when he was gone.

In the final weeks in the middle room, cared for so lovingly by his wife and sons, Noel's consciousness faded. Hospice staff helped during the final days. Noel died on 8 December 2003, the feast of the Immaculate Conception of the Blessed Virgin Mary.

## Funeral

The following evening, the Oblate Church in Inchicore was not big enough for all who turned up for the removal. Two auxiliary bishops of Dublin, Eamonn Walsh and Ray Field, were present along with hundreds of other mourners. Later that evening, Dillon's public house overflowed with mourners.

The next morning, 10 December, International Human Rights Day, Fr Brian Power was the chief celebrant at the funeral Mass. Then resident in the Sue Ryder Retirement Home in Dalkey, the seventy-three-year-old priest was not as robust as he had been when, as a curate in St Michael's parish, his friendship with Noel was born. At the start of Mass, Brian placed his walking stick noisily on the altar. Then, and later in his homily, it was clear how upset he was at Noel's untimely passing. Brian's sorrow resonated with the mood of many in the congregation. Former St Vincent's club member and future Lord Mayor of Dublin Catherine Byrne's singing reverberated throughout the church and heightened the atmosphere. SVP President Brian O'Reilly spoke convincingly about Noel's contribution to Irish life. It was a memorable and prayerful occasion. Mourners included family and friends, people from the youth club years, and those he met through the probation and welfare service. SVP members from every region in Ireland, along with Jim O'Connor and Iain McTurk, SVP presidents from England and Scotland respectively, were also present. Noel's remains were buried in Esker Cemetery, Lucan

# Chapter 30
## Keeping the Memory Alive

Noel Clear's legacy is an enormous one. At one level, he was an ordinary person with a job and a family who volunteered a few hours each week. On the other hand, his commitment ran deep and 'a few hours' expanded to fill much of his spare time. Noel was a very private person who preferred to speak through action rather than words. Like many SVP members, he was driven by an authentic religious faith. As Pope Francis has remarked: 'An authentic faith – which is never comfortable or completely personal – always involves a deep desire to change the world, to transmit values, to leave this earth somehow better that we found it.'[1]

Within his immediate family, Noel's memory is lovingly sustained especially by his dignified and thoughtful brothers, Tony and Seán, his intelligent and devoted wife Anne and their children and families. The SVP now has a more nuanced view of the balance between charity and justice, of the dignity of each individual and of human solidarity.

For many who knew him, Noel's appreciation of human and divine motivations for his work was clear. He lived the Vincentian

---

1. Pope Francis, Apostolic Exhortation, *Evangelii Gaudium*, 183.

vocation in his daily actions. This is the challenge that every SVP member faces: how to go beyond dispositions of sympathy in the face of poverty and injustices. As Noel might have said, 'yes, we are angry at the injustice we see but what are we going to do about it?' Echoes of Noel's insights and motivations are reflected today in many SVP members.

### De Paul volunteer award

A year after Noel's death, Archbishop Diarmuid Martin, when launching the annual report of the De Paul Trust at an event in Croke Park, presented Frances McCarthy with the 'volunteer of the year' award for her work with the Clancy Nightshelter. This award was also designated 'in Memory of Mr Noel Clear'.

### A Dublin honour

Each year since 1989, the Lord Mayor of the City of Dublin pays tribute to a small number of people who have performed exceptional service to the citizens of the capital. Award recipients have included an impressive range of sportspeople, cultural figures and social activists.[2]

'Trying to pick four people from a population of over a million people is very difficult,' says one former Lord Mayor, adding 'and, of course, you offend so many by leaving them out'. When Lord Mayor Catherine Byrne sat down to choose recipients for 2006,

---

2. Recipients of the Lord Mayor's Awards have included sportspeople Ronnie Delany, Eamonn Coughlan, Kevin Moran, Charlie Redmond, Padraig Harrington, Brian Kerr, Ken Doherty and Brian O'Driscoll, cultural figures Maeve Binchy, Jim Sheridan, Neil Jordan, Donal McCann, Brenda Fricker, Mary Black, Gay Byrne, Carolyn Swift, Des Keogh and Rosaleen Linehan, social activists Alice Leahy, Fr Michael Mernagh, Tom Hyland, Cathleen O'Neill, Sr Consilio and Sr Stanislaus Kennedy. Groups that have been honoured include Our Lady's Hospice in Harold's Cross, the Ruhama Women's Project and the Irish Foundation for Torture Survivors.

the first name on her list was Noel Clear. Even though Noel had died in 2003, she still wanted his contribution acknowledged.

'I believe this man changed the course of many people's lives, especially mine,' she told guests in the Round Room in the Mansion House among whom were Anne, Rory, Alan and Conor. Catherine Byrne recalled an incident when she was eight years of age and wanted to join the local St Vincent's Club in Inchicore. Noel explained that it was a boys' club and she couldn't join. However, the future politician did not take 'no' for an answer and persisted until the committee eventually decided to allow girls join the club. 'That determined young woman will go far,' remarked the perceptive Noel at the time.

The Lord Mayor continued: 'for many children in my parish the only holiday they had was with the youth club. We spend many a happy holiday in Carne, Skerries, Rathangan and Rathdrum where the greatest of care was given by Noel and many other leaders'. She also recalled how 'Vincent's' played an important role in keeping her and others out of trouble. Catherine herself went on to become a voluntary youth leader in the club.

As well as honouring his contribution to Inchicore, the Lord Mayor stressed Noel's national role. 'For over fifty years Noel was a visionary, working and challenging social disadvantage in the city, especially during his years as National President of the Society of St Vincent de Paul. Noel's life was dedicated to those in his community and in the city who, in many ways, had been left behind, and where in many homes, there was little food but always a listening ear from Noel. Noel became a friendly face for St Vincent de Paul in the community,' she said. Describing Noel as 'truly, an ordinary person doing extraordinary things', the Lord Mayor said that it was 'with a great sense of pride and respect' that she was presenting the award to Noel's widow, Anne.

For Anne, widowed in her fifties, it was a night of mixed emotions. 'Of course, I was very proud. It was great to see his contribution acknowledged in that way. But there was also great sadness that Noel wasn't there himself.'

## Remembering

Outside, Storm Desmond is howling across the country, gusting leaves which gather in shores and cause flash flooding. Inside number fifty Tyrconnell Road, some of Noel's family are gathering on this cold December night to mark the twelfth anniversary of his death. It's been an annual event since 2004. This year it's obvious how much Noel and Anne's grandchildren have advanced beyond the baby stage. Young Noel is now seven, and Katie, Jack and Cian are also intrigued at the gathering around the table. They peer curiously as Vincentian priest Fr Seán Farrell prepares for Mass. As he begins, Seán acknowledges the children, telling the intimate congregation how, 'I knew your grandfather, admired him greatly. To work with him on various committees was a privilege,' he pauses, catches the eyes of the adults and adds, 'even if we had disagreements which I often didn't win.' A collective knowing smile spreads across the faces of Anne, Rory, his wife Kathryn, Alan, his wife Niamh, Conor and the small number of family friends in the room.

Throughout the Mass, many themes resonate with aspects of Noel's life: mercy, compassion, safety, trust, faith, hope, love, service. At the prayers of the faithful, his grandson Noel reads prayers he had written for the occasion. How values and priorities get passed from generation to generation are reflected in young Noel's concerns, for the poor, for homeless people, for those who died in the Paris bombing, for the sick and 'for all those who have died especially Grandad Noel.'

After Mass, when refreshments were enjoyed and the well-behaved grandchildren headed for their beds, a rich, wide-ranging and lively discussion ensued. A central theme was social and Church-related changes that had taken place during Noel's lifetime and how various people, including those present, have responded to these changes. Towards the end, some interesting parallels were made between Noel's life and that of Jorge Bergoglio. The Argentinian Pope Francis, born a year earlier than Noel, is very driven by a strong faith rooted in values of compassion and mercy, two of Noel's defining qualities. A telling phrase from the encyclical *Laudato Si'* – '... hear the cry of the earth and hear the cry of the poor' – resonates. The pope's approach to organisational reform is to continually remind people to focus on the core mission of the Church. In *Evangelii Gaudium, Joy of the Gospel,* he writes: 'Before all else, the Gospel invites us to respond to the love of God who saves us, to go forth from ourselves and to seek the good in others.' Not that Francis shied away from naming some of the organisational problems he sees, including reducing the 'church to a nest protecting our mediocrity'.

### The Traveller

Noel's journey from 1937 to 2003 was one through a changing society. 'Nationalist', 'Gaelic' and 'Catholic' identities went through various cycles, fashions and understandings. The Troubles in Northern Ireland challenged the republican beliefs of many. Irish language policy and practice never quite rhymed the reality with the rhetoric. The GAA ban on foreign games gave way to less exclusive thinking. Catholicism underwent a radical reimagining at the Vatican Council and then, in the light of clerical sexual abuse and cover up, the institution's credibility was severely dented. Inward migration contributed to a more pluralist Ireland. A wealthier Ireland developed alongside increased inequalities.

Noel struggled with all these issues and identities, positioning and re-positioning himself.

Described variously as mediator, peacemaker, loyal to so many people but angry at injustice, 'a lovely man' who could laugh at his own shortcomings, an old-fashioned gentleman, a leader without an ego, gifted organiser, decision-maker, problem solver, and, in the words of his friend and former colleague Tom Gilmore 'a sort of taken-for-granted individual' who never made a compliment of doing anything and so made it awfully easy to ask.

Noel's early family life laid a strong foundation. Belief in his own dignity and that of every other human being was central. A bright, optimistic view of life and its possibilities was tempered by a recognition of gratitude. The phrase 'there but for the grace of God go I' catches a non-judgemental recognition that circumstances can shape and misshape lives. Noel the Christian saw himself attempting to be faithful to the memory of Jesus, the humble carpenter and itinerant preacher from Nazareth who went about doing good. He drew inspiration from the Gospels which he read carefully and took seriously.

When talking about Noel, some use the word 'saint'. When someone suggested to the American Catholic activist Dorothy Day[3] that she was a saint, her reply was: 'Don't call me a saint. I don't want to be dismissed so easily.' It's a sentiment you could imagine Noel expressing. His life also resonates with a saying attributed to that great champion of the poor, St Francis of Assisi: 'Preach the Gospel at all times and, if necessary, use words.'

---

3. Dorothy Day (1897–1980) was a journalist and social activist who converted to Catholicism. She co-founded the newspaper the *Catholic Worker* in 1933. In his address to the United States Congress in September 2015, Pope Francis cited her, along with Abraham Lincoln, Martin Luther King Junior and Thomas Merton as four exemplary Americans.

His good friend Jerry O'Sullivan is effusive about Noel. He says:

I have no doubt that I had the privilege of working with a genuine saint, a man chosen by God to do great work, who gave me an opportunity to make so many friends in Dublin, to do something that today represents the happiest achievement of my life, to have reached this age still sharing the gift of faith in Jesus, our Saviour.

Jerry continues:

His whole life, including the years he worked in the prison service, was a life of dedication to the needy, the youth searching for a meaning in life, the men and women who had fallen foul of the laws of the country. His was a life of a true patriot, a genuine believer, a lover of all that is good and noble, a man dedicated to service and sharing.

Just as I was concluding this account, a message from Pope Francis had a strong impact. Like more than ten million others I follow him on Twitter (@Pontifex) and in early June 2017 he tweeted: 'The Church needs everyday saints, those of ordinary life carried out with coherence.'

I thought of Noel and that word 'coherence' struck home. Coherence characterised Noel so well.

## Challenges

In the years since Noel died, the challenges presented to those aspiring to live as Christians championing charity and justice have become more complex. Christianity has moved from a mainstream position of power and influence to a more marginal one. Many see this as bringing a welcome purification, a clarity, a focus and a return to core values. Being part of a counter-cultural movement can bring its own energy and grace. On the other hand, a strident secularism can appear to disregard organisations like the SVP and volunteers like Noel.

Some members fear that, in accommodating itself to modern society, the SVP is paring itself down to a social activist organisation, drifting from its spiritual, religious and church roots. Another view recognises the SVP as a component of Church life relatively unsullied by scandal and mediocrity, a living response to the core Christian invitation to 'love your neighbour', manifesting strong solidarity with marginalised people, not unduly weighed down with historical baggage. Indeed, such a focus on 'back to basics' represents one way forward for a discredited and demoralized Church.

Historically, Irish people identified strongly with poor people at home and abroad. Even if subdued, memory of the Famine in the middle of the nineteenth century is never far from the surface. It's as if we have had an almost instinctive identification with the oppressed, the underdogs, the victims. Support across age, gender, social class and other interest groups for agencies such as the Society of St Vincent de Paul, Trocaire, Concern, Christian Aid, the Peter McVerry Trust reinforces this.

As Noel frequently asserted, Ireland is a rich country. We have the resources to eliminate poverty. However, as some individuals become relatively rich, complacency, hubris and a forgetfulness of the past become real dangers. An unequivocal commitment to social justice has implications for one's own wallet, purse, tax bill and general lifestyle. The 'good news' of the Gospels is shared not only in word but in action. Noel embodied those Gospel values, of bringing 'good news to the poor'.

I try to imagine Noel reading what has been written here. I see him wishing to deflect attention away from himself towards 'the issues' and people in distress. I suspect that, if he compared living and working conditions in Ireland today with the time when he began to recognise those challenges in Keogh Square, he would acknowledge the improvements, indeed the social transformation that has taken place. But I also hear him posing uncomfortable questions, about children going to bed hungry, people sleeping on Dublin's streets, homeless families housed in hotels, the dearth of social housing, the persistence of educational disadvantage and health waiting lists, the increased use of guns, the ongoing scourge of drug abuse, the scandal of direct provision, the marginalisation of refugees and asylum seekers, the obscenity of global inequalities. Noel's persistent question 'Could we be doing more?' rings out clearly, as relevant today as it was during his lifetime.